NO NIGGERS IN MY CORPS

The true story of how a group of racist white high school JROTC cadets plotted to drive their black instructor out of their school

by Master Sergeant Cardelle Anthony Hopkins, USAF, Ret.

DEDICATION

Dedicated to the loving memory of Grandma Ruth, Grandma Annie, Grand Daddy John, and Grand Daddy Charlie. Forever in our hearts.

Copyright © 2022 by Cardelle Anthony Hopkins

Publishing all rights reserved worldwide. All rights reserved as sole property of the author.

The author guarantees all content is original and does not infringe upon the legal rights of any other person or work.

No part of this book may be reproduced, stored in a retrieval system, or transmitted in any form or by any means, without expressed written permission of the author.

Edited by Lil Barcaski and Linda Hinkle

Published by: GWN Publishing

www.GWNPublishing.com

Cover Design: Kristina Conatser Captured by KC Design

ISBN: 979-8-9859746-0-7 Kindle
ISBN: 978-0-578-28498-9 Print

CONTENTS

Introduction 7

JROTC: Discovering My Path. 11

Getting the Dream Job. 17

New Job – New Challenges 25

A Lesson in the Levels of Multifaceted Discrimination . . .33

Pops of Prejudice Crack the Foundation. 39

A Fresh Start Turns Sour 47

Hateful Alt Right Words Spewed on Instagram and in Print . .53

Expected vs Actual Response. 61

Outrage and Support .69

Resolution. 81

An Interview with Daniel Smith, Teacher and Advocate . .93

Appendix 99

Acknowledgments 117

About the Author 119

Names of certain individuals have been changed to protect their privacy. All events are described from the author's perspective and/or recollection. The author does not know how other individuals thought or regarded other people, and his opinion(s) of those interactions are just that – only his opinion.

INTRODUCTION

Growing up, we were raised to be very patriotic. I always knew that I would spend a good portion of my life serving our country. Both my mother and father instilled in us kids a great pride to be Americans. My younger brother, Michael, served in the Army in the famous 101st Airborne Division. My baby sister married an Army man and raised three children, one of whom served in the Army as well.

Growing up as an "Army brat" and then spending 23 years on my adult life in the USAF, I was shielded from a lot of the racism that existed in the United States. For the bulk of my life, I legitimately thought that all Americans were proud and patriotic like our family. I knew there were some Americans out there that hated the country. However, I thought they were just misinformed. Like many, I turned out to be the one who was uninformed about just how vile and disgusting racism can be, especially when it happens to you.

Recently, while teaching Air Force JROTC (AFJROTC) at a school in Florida, I was introduced to racist behavior firsthand. I had never experienced such racist behavior in my entire life. It was a wake-up call for me. I was forced to take notice to a change that I see occurring within our country at many levels, a change and shift towards white nationalism at the high school JROTC level. I wanted to write a book about my encounter with racism as a Veteran and an AFJROTC instructor. My goal is to help prevent what happened to me from happening to any other JROTC Instructor or any teacher at all.

When people read this book, I want them to remember that, as a country, we are better than the racists that brings us down. I want the reader to remember that the men and women who sign up to defend this country are doing so regardless of race, gender, sexual orientation, or ethnicity. If we can teach tolerance in places such as high school JROTC, we will continue to rise and be all that we can be as a nation.

For me, personally, I know that we are stronger as a country when we are more accepting of others who are different than us. At the end of the day, America is stronger when we stand side by side as Americans.

My father has always been my hero. To this day, I am still impressed by his relentless work ethic. His integrity, service before self, and excellence in all he does. My siblings and I refer to him as Pop.

Pop's life story is interesting and amazing. He grew up in the deep South in the 1960's in Greenville, North Carolina. During his late teen years, he was not very fond of the country and how it treated black folks. Somewhere around 18 years old, prior to my birth, he joined the Black Panther Party, a revolutionary party founded in 1966. The party was known for several of its beliefs including having Marxist views. However, near the Black Panther's peak years, the Vietnam War brought the military draft to many African-American communities, effectively stymying the growth of the movement.

Introduction

In 1967, Pop was drafted by the United States Army. Pops was not happy going to war for a country that he felt did not love him. Patriotism was not his top priority at that point in time. Anger at the system was more his feeling. How did a country that treated a segment of its people so cruelly expect those same people to fight and/or die for the same country? Faced with possible jail time, Pop accepted the challenge and was subsequently sent to fight in Vietnam. While in Vietnam, he lost several friends in battle and, in action, he was sprayed with Agent Orange.

Upon returning from Vietnam, Pop's entire outlook changed. The Vietnam experience changed his view of service to the U.S. Army and the U.S. Constitution. His loyalty to the men and women of the U.S. military increased by leaps and bounds. Over time, his loyalty and dedication to the United States grew as well. My father completely bought into the American Dream. He dreamed of a good life with his family. Every day, we reaped the benefits of his hard work. As young military brats, my sister, brother, and I had the opportunity to travel the world with my parents. I spent the first 21 years of my life living on or near Army installations, two of which assignments were overseas in Germany.

Pop spent 26 years in the U.S. Army. Upon retirement from the Army, he spent 20 years teaching as an Army JROTC Instructor. He became one of the most patriotic people I have ever met in my entire life. It was no surprise to my family when I enlisted into the United States military. Although I chose the United States Air Force (USAF) instead of the United States Army. I chose to serve just like Pop did. I spent 23 years on active duty. I always planned to pattern my life after my father's. After all, in my opinion, Pop created a blueprint for success, and I decided to follow his same roadmap.

NO NIGGERS IN MY CORPS

While on active duty and stationed at MacDill Air Force Base in Tampa, Florida, I had the opportunity to watch Pop's high school JROTC team compete in a national drill meet. His cadets from Miami Senior High School were phenomenal. They scored high in the competitions and won several trophies. All of Pop's cadets were very professional and well-spoken 9th through 12th grade high school kids who showed extreme maturity.

I asked them how they had become so professional and driven. They all credited my Pop, aka Sergeant Hopkins for pushing and training them to be the best citizens that they could possibly be.

That's when I first knew that I wanted to become an Air Force JROTC Instructor. After retiring from the Air Force and obtaining my bachelor's degree, I got hired at Ashley Ridge High School in Summerville, South Carolina as a certified JROTC Instructor just like Pop. Little did I know that my journey as a JROTC Instructor would start out like Pop's but would end up being quite a different experience.

CHAPTER 1

JROTC: DISCOVERING MY PATH

While on active duty and stationed at MacDill Air Force Base in Tampa, Florida, I drove out to Lakeland, Florida to watch my father's high school Army JROTC team compete in a national drill meet. His cadets from Miami Senior High School were phenomenal. They scored off the charts in all the drill related competitions and won several trophies. Pop's cadets were very professional and well spoken. These kids were anywhere from 9th to 12th grade high school students, yet they showed extreme maturity.

I asked them how they had become so professional and driven. They all credited my Pop (aka First Sergeant Hopkins) for pushing and training them to be the best citizens that they could possibly be. Right then, I knew that I wanted to be an Air Force JROTC Instructor at some point in the future and that I would work toward that goal as soon as possible.

I retired from the Air Force in 2013, knowing that I wanted to teach Air Force JROTC. However, I did not have a degree at the time, so I was unable to apply for a JROTC position. The requirements for teaching Air Force JROTC included being retired from the Air Force with 20 or more years of service – check – and hold a bachelor's degree in any field of study – my new goal.

I had not completed my bachelor's degree and still had many hours to go in order to graduate. I began attending Saint Leo University at night and on the weekends while working full time at the Social Security Administration. Fortunately, I had taken some classes while I was still on active duty. However, I was only starting my second year of college upon my retirement from the Air Force. I had been studying Criminal Justice prior to retiring from the Air Force, so I continued in that area of study.

In 2016, I finally graduated from Saint Leo University with a bachelor's degree in Criminal Justice and a minor in Homeland Security. It was a point of pride that I was the first person in my immediate family to graduate from college. Now I was ready to pursue my dream of becoming a JROTC instructor like my father.

After completing all the requirements, I searched out AFJROTC jobs in Florida. At the time, there were no jobs available in the entire state. I widened by search to include jobs that might be available high schools in Georgia. Still no luck, as there were no openings in that neighboring state either. I was reluctant to search any further as I did not want to get too far away from the Tampa area. Tampa Bay is and was my home since 2002 when stationed at MacDill Airforce Base. There are only a few bases that are near big cities, and MacDill is also on the water, which both I and my family loved. I wanted to be close to home and still pursue my career goal.

JROTC: Discovering My Path

My dad had already retired from teaching Army JROTC in Miami, and he and my mother had moved back to Columbia, SC, so I decided to take a peek at job openings in South Carolina. There was one opening at a school called Ashley Ridge High School in Summerville, South Carolina, a suburb of Charleston, SC. After consulting with my wife and sons, I decided to notify the Air Force that I was interested in the position. The Air Force has a process in place whereby they won't typically send your name to the principal of a school to fill a position until there are at least six applicants for the one position. It varies a bit on that rule, but they typically stick to it. In my case, there were already five other applicants plus me, making me number six. Of all the applicants, I was the junior of the group and the only one with absolutely no teaching experience. However, I was so enthused about the opportunity that I went forward with my application.

Prior to leaving for the interview, my wife and I agreed that if hired, I would use this opportunity as a gauge to see if teaching JROTC was a good fit for me. Because I was the junior of the six applicants, I guessed that I probably wouldn't get the job.

I later discovered, long after I was hired for the job, why Major Drake chose me. He's Caucasian and a bit older. He had a rough time communicating and interacting with the young African-American males in the group. Hiring me was his olive branch to diversity. African-American kids, especially those who come from families that are well off, don't typically take JROTC. Air Force JROTC involves scholarship opportunities, but even so, black folks don't like working for the man. To those families, it felt as though they were putting their kids into the military. They didn't get that JROTC is not a breeding ground for recruiting kids into service. Major Drake wanted to have a better line of communication between him and his black students, thus I would be given a chance that I might otherwise not have been given.

I can only assume I was one of the few, if not the only, African-American applicant and the lowest in rank. I left the Air Force as a Master Sergeant, which means I am considered a non-commissioned officer. My dad was also an enlisted man his whole career.

He would make a joke when someone called him sir. "Don't call me sir, I work for a living," he would jest. My dad was in essence a blue-collar, hardworking, regular guy. I admired that about him amongst other things. It may be why I never sought to become a commissioned officer. Other than the pay raise, being an officer didn't appeal to me. I liked being on the ground with the troops. It was another appeal to working with the JROTC. I got to be with the kids be on the ground.

It can be hard for the younger JROTC cadets to connect with senior instructors. Those officers are commissioned officers, and it may feel like there is a great emotional distance from them for high school students. Add in the fact of race, and you create an even greater distance.

Major Drake was old school southern, grew up in the south, and attended the Citadel. Working at this school basically meant he had come home to his roots.

Early the Sunday morning before my interview, my 18-year-old son and I left Tampa for our road trip to South Carolina. I decided to take the scenic route. I had spent some time in the deep South, but my son had not, so I thought that we would do some sightseeing while we traveled. As we drove the back road highways of the deep South, we passed a few cotton fields and rice fields. We were far from the faster paced metropolitan lifestyle of Tampa.

After passing our second cotton field, my son asked me if I was sure that I wanted to do this. I, of course, said yes, though I had some trepidation about what working in this environment might bring. I had lived in the south much of my life. I knew the pitfalls of prejudice that came with the territory, but times had changed, and I was hopeful that my experience, should I by some miracle be hired, would be a positive one.

Monday morning, on the way to Ashley Ridge High School (ARHS), we came up through Charleston, SC. To my son, downtown Charleston had an antebellum feel to it. He said that the city reminded him of the "days of slavery." He quickly apologized for his outburst and said he was not trying to talk me out of the interview. About 10 miles or so from the school, we passed a sign for another plantation. It was our fourth plantation of the day, Magnolia Plantation. My son just looked at me with a sarcastic smile.

During my teen years, my father was stationed at Fort Jackson Army Base in Columbia, South Carolina. On several occasions, we traveled down to Charleston to visit friends. I never did much sightseeing during those visits. Later on, my parents moved down to Charleston. I enjoyed visiting them, however, I still didn't do any sightseeing. At that time, I was not interested in the historical aspects of the city whatsoever.

When I took the job at Ashley Ridge High School, it happened to be less than 20 minutes from the Charleston Air Force Base. Three to four times per week, I visited the gym on the Air Force base. For the first six or seven months, I passed the Magnolia Plantation many times on my way to and from Charleston and/or the Air Force base. Finally, with a few weeks remaining in the school year, I randomly decided to visit the Magnolia Plantation. I was not a big fan of anything with the word "plantation" in its title, but I decided to check it out.

As I arrived, the first thing that I noticed was that I was the only African-American tourist there at that specific time. I told myself that there had to be other African-Americans touring the property besides me. Strangely enough, I spent the entire time looking for another African-American tourist. I am certain that there are other African-Americans that are curious about life on a plantation in the deep South, but at that particular time, it appeared I was the only African-American there, besides the guides and staff. Nonetheless, I ventured on.

The gardens were very beautiful and well groomed, and the huge plantation home was breathtaking. However, after hearing the guide tell the history of how the enslaved people were treated, I soon lost my appreciation of the beautiful gardens and the large plantation home as its meaning was lost in what it represented, a part of our nation's history that was very disturbing and dark. Although, the tour was very interesting and informative, I left feeling angry, but more so, saddened at how the enslaved people were treated. I was, however, impressed at their ability to survive the often harsh and unforgiving life as slaves in the deep South. I was glad that I had gone to the Magnolia Plantation. It taught me several things that I had not learned in school about the Antebellum South, things that are rarely, if ever, taught in the classrooms of America today or ever.

CHAPTER 2

GETTING THE DREAM JOB

As we pulled up to the school for my interview, my stomach started to churn with pent-up nervousness. I had no idea what to expect. When I got out of the car, a Chief Master Sergeant (Chief) in his service dress uniform was heading toward his car.

Chief Master Sergeant is the highest-ranking enlisted rank. He smiled at me and asked if I was here for the interview. I said yes. He politely said good luck. I asked him if he was here for the interview as well. He said he was. He told me that he had been teaching JROTC for 10 years up North and was trying to get back home to the Charleston area. I responded good luck to him as well and waved as he drove off.

Although I am very confident in my abilities, my confidence level dropped tremendously. The Chief was polite, but he was a seasoned instructor and a freakin' Chief Master Sergeant! My odds of landing this job were rapidly shrinking.

NO NIGGERS IN MY CORPS

I was an hour early for the interview. While I walked around trying to stay loose and relaxed, a car pulled up next to me. It was another Chief. He asked if I worked at the school. I told him no. He apologized and said he mistook me being in uniform out in front of the school, thinking perhaps I was there to greet the applicants for the JROTC position. I informed him that I, too, was one of the applicants, I was just way early. We both laughed. He said, "Yep, that's how the Air Force rolls, always ahead of schedule."

He asked how long I had been teaching. I told him that I had never taught high school at all. He responded he hadn't either. He had only been retired from active-duty status for a few weeks, and it turned out he was from Florida as well. I wished him good luck. As he walked into the building, my son sarcastically said to me "Pop, you got some serious competition today. All these dudes are Chiefs."

In a little while, the second Chief walked out, shook my hand, and said good luck. Two young cadet Colonels walked out to greet me. I hadn't seen them earlier. They were both high school seniors and had just arrived at the school. They asked if I was ready to go back to the office for the interview. I set my shoulders back and told them I was.

As my son headed back to the car, he turned and said, "Hey, Pop. You got this bro." One of the cadet Colonels asked if that was my son, and I shook my head in the affirmative. He shouted to my son, "Excuse me. Why don't you come on back as well? You can hang out with us while your dad does his interview."

My son turned and jogged back to the school to join our little group.

Both cadets were the same age as my son. They immediately started talking sports and cars. I had to intervene to remind then I had to get to my interview.

"Listen, young men, I love cars, too. However, I would love to get back there for the interview before I'm late."

They were laughing when the senior instructor, Major Drake, came out looking for us.

"I see you've met the twins," he said.

I was puzzled. I responded, "the twins, sir?" as the two cadets looked nothing alike. Major Drake said, "They're not really twins but twins in rank."

They were the Cadet Corps leaders: Commander Cadet Colonel Richards, and Deputy Commander Cadet Andrews. Both young men were sharp, polite, and well-spoken.

As Major Drake took me back for the interview, my confidence began to return and thanks to the two Cadet Colonels, my nerves were calmer too. When I walked into the conference room, there were two assistant principals already seated at the table. Major Drake started the interview. He introduced everyone. The first interviewer asked me if I would tell them a little bit about myself. Ten minutes later, I noticed that they were all starting to check their watches. I realized that I had been talking far too long. My mouth was dry, and I seemed to have lost the attention of all three attendees. Major Drake gave me a quick Air Force nod to wrap it up, and my confidence sunk again.

Then, it was Major Drake's turn to speak. He asked why I wanted to teach JROTC. No joke, 10 minutes later, he was giving me the same Air Force nod to wrap it up. My nerves got the best of me, and I couldn't seem to stop myself from over-explaining.

I was convinced that I blew the interview. One of the assistant principals said she had two questions, but I had answered both questions during my "briefing." They all laughed. I didn't know whether to laugh or not, so I just sat, finally quietly, and smiled. The other assistant principal said something similar that I had already answered her questions too. Since we were so far ahead of schedule and I was the last interview for the day, they asked if I had any questions for them. Like clockwork, 10 minutes later, Major Drake was giving me the wrap-it up nod.

After the interview, the two Cadet Colonels and Major Drake had no further responsibilities, so they graciously offered to take my son and I on a tour of the campus and the JROTC unit as well. It turned out to be a wonderful experience. However, I was quite certain I had probably bombed the interview. Major Drake was very businesslike as it pertained to the interview. He only said that they all loved my enthusiasm.

When we got back to Tampa, I checked the Air Force portal. There were two Florida high schools that had JROTC openings. One in Miami and one in Jacksonville. Neither school had a Senior Instructor at the time, so I was a little hesitant to apply being that I was brand new to the JROTC sphere.

The following Tuesday morning, Major Drake called me to let me know that all the interviews had concluded. He asked if I had any other interviews scheduled. I told him about the two in Florida, but I said that I was hoping to join his team. I asked him why he wanted to know about my other interviews.

"I can't tell you that you got the job, but don't go to the other interviews," he replied.

I knew what that meant, and I was ecstatic!

Needless to say, I was offered the job and I took it. It was a great school. Major Drake and Master Sergeant McDowell ran a tight ship. I was assigned roughly 70 freshman cadets and 20 senior cadets. With almost 200 cadets, Ashley Ridge JROTC was the epitome of Air Force JROTC led by Major Drake, a Citadel graduate who had helped start the program at ARHS. I felt honored and blessed to have been given this opportunity.

I was also given the additional duty of Drill Team Supervisor and was included in some very cool outings, including a two-week Citadel Summer Camp for AFJROTC students from around the country, which was held in Charleston.

Having lived in the South for a good while as a teen and having graduated from a high school in Columbia, SC, I was very familiar with all of the racial tensions, nuances and stereotypes of life in the deep South. I braced myself for any racial animus that might transpire while I was there.

To my surprise, the entire year that I was there was nothing but routine. We put a bunch of cadets into college and planned for the next school year. I really enjoyed my experience with Major Drake at ARHS. Unfortunately, due to an unforeseen family situation, I had to return to Tampa at the end of the 2017 school year. My wife was diagnosed with a severe case of Grave's disease. They caught it early on, but she had to undergo very difficult treatments. My sons, one a teen and one a tween, needed me to be home, as did my wife. Reluctantly, I had to leave my position for one much closer to home and there were no JROTC positions that fit that bill.

NO NIGGERS IN MY CORPS

It was hard to say goodbye to the cadets under my tutelage. However, I knew I had found my new dream career of being an Air Force JROTC Instructor and that eventually I would find my way back to it.

So, I went to work for the department of juvenile justice as a juvenile probation officer. It fit with my education and allowed me to be close to home. I had a case load of 15 kids. I had to make sure they showed up for their court dates and completed their community service.

While it wasn't my dream job, it allowed me to deal with teenagers, and I had a few very interesting experiences. One such case was a young man that, I hate to admit, got what he deserved based on his bad behavior. He was sitting on a park bench with his girlfriend in a little neighborhood park in Temple Terrace, a small city outside of Tampa. They were watching as a mom tossed a ball back and forth with her young son. Mom had no throwing arm, and the kid was complaining to her that she couldn't throw.

The young man asked her if she wanted him to play ball with her son, and she said she would appreciate it if he did. Being far too trusting, she said she was going to use the rest room and left not only her child with this seemingly nice young man, but her purse on the bench beside him. In her short absence, the young man in question stole her money and even her car, using the keys he found in the purse.

Little did he know that the woman was a former district attorney. To add insult to injury, he committed a robbery in her car. The former D.A. made sure he and his friend were duly prosecuted, and he wound up on my list.

In another case, I worked with a kid who had been driving in a car with two other kids. They picked up one more to make it four. After an altercation, he shot the newcomer but missed and hit a person in the house behind his intended victim. At 16, he was charged with attempted murder.

Kids are spontaneous and they often do stupid things.

One kid had been in the system since he was 11 years old, mainly for drug abuse. I was dealing with him at age 17. I went to his house to see if I could get a clean drug test and get him out of the system. When I got there, I realized that everyone in the entire house was smoking pot or doing drugs. He couldn't stay away from it.

Of the 15 kids I worked with, only two were white kids – one from a super wealthy family whose parents had the money to stay out of the system. The judge allowed the mom to be the one to look after him. I could only check on him once a week. When you talked to this kid, he seemed to have it together. He had a lucrative business of his own cutting grass for many families in his neighborhood, went to school, and lived at home. His crime was having date raped a 15-year-old girl. He sodomized her and left her naked in the street. His parents paid off the girl's parents not to make this a big deal out the incident. They paid for expensive lawyers to get him off the hook. He was not into drugs, and he was not caught doing anything else at that time, so he got off easy, but I always wondered – what will he turn out to be?

The other white kid was likeable. His mom and dad knew he smoked pot, but he eventually graduated to other drugs. Frustrated with his behavior, his dad tried to roughhouse him, and the son attacked the dad with mom standing there. He was much bigger than his dad, but the father managed to push his son off of him, causing the boy's face to be messed up in the tussle. Mom told the authorities that her son had attacked his father, so I got him as his probation officer.

The other 13 of my kids were black. Was it a matter of race or class? If they were white, would they have been there? Kids go through the JAC – Juvenile Assessment Center – up to the age of 17. They all get processed through this. Most of the issues that occur happen in school, mostly fights.

The toughest one for me to swallow was when a young black kid spit on another kid, in fact, another black kid. An officer brought him into the JAC. All he had done was spit on the other kid, and now he was in the system. This sort of incident usually starts with bringing the parents into the school and an apology by the offending kid with a promise from the parents that he or she would be harshly dealt with at home.

In this case, the officer was white. Would he have brought a white kid in for the same minor offense? That single mistake started this kid's journey into the court system.

This experience taught me a lot about dealing with kids but even seeing some of the imbalance and injustice in the system did not prepare me for what I would experience when I got my next JROTC position.

CHAPTER 3

NEW JOB – NEW CHALLENGES
THURSDAY, JULY 26, 2018

It was the usual hot and muggy summer day. We left Tampa and headed up Interstate-4 (I-4). Traffic would prove to be more of a challenge than the job interview. Luckily, I-4 traffic improved a bit as we approached downtown Orlando. Pulling into Altamonte Springs city limits, I was pleasantly surprised by the size and activity of the city. It was nothing like I thought it would be. I had only seen Altamonte Springs on a map. I assumed that it was a sleepy bedroom community on the outskirts of Orlando. Much to my surprise, it was a bustling city. As we drove towards Lake Brantley High School, I felt a certain warmness about the place.

My interview for the Air Force JROTC (AFJROTC) instructor position was scheduled for 2:00 p.m. and took place during the summer break, so school was still out. Both my wife and two sons accompanied me on the trip. We arrived at Lake Brantley High School at 1:15 p.m., ahead of schedule as always.

I called the Assistant Principal, Mrs. Douglas, to let her know that I was early and was outside waiting. Mrs. Douglas was the facilitator of the interview. The Senior JROTC Instructor, Major Powers, greeted me at the gate. As he spoke to me, I immediately noted his thick Southern accent. I also noticed that although he was in his semi-formal service dress, an Air Force uniform, he was not wearing the mandatory black oxford-style military shoes mandated for the blue semi-formal uniform. He was wearing black gym shoes. In my 23 years of military service, I had never seen this before. Nonetheless, I did not make a big deal out of it. I just made a mental note to myself that he had the audacity to wear sneakers with his semi- formal uniform. I figured it was one of those out of sight, out of mind situations. Headquarters was not around to look over his shoulder kind of thing. Also at the interview was the instructor that I would soon be replacing, Master Sergeant Dupree. He was the epitome of the hard-charging Senior Non-Commissioned Officer (SNCO) that I was familiar with from my active duty days. Master Sergeant Dupree had recently earned his master's degree. While teaching AFJROTC, he had attended school at night and on the weekends. He was your typical blue color SNCO but was now moving on to be an administrator at a local middle school in the area.

The interview went outstandingly well. I felt good about it from beginning to end. After the interview, we spent a few minutes talking about sports and restaurants. It felt as if I had known them all for some time, even though we had just met.

After the interview, Major Powers gave my wife and I a tour of the entire high school. Major Powers and my wife hit it off very well. She was fascinated by his deep Mississippi drawl. She told me that he sounded like a character from the movie, "Gone with The Wind." His words flowed slow and steady, like the cadence of a Southern Baptist minister. At one point during

New Job – New Challenges

the interview, MSgt Dupree uttered, "Amen, Brother," as Major Powers finished one of his selling points. As a matter of fact, I assumed that Major Powers might have had some experience at preaching as well. I found the entire interview and tour to be very warm and sincere. I got very positive vibes from the experience, so much so that I cancelled my interviews in both Jacksonville and Miami.

In retrospect, it was silly to cancel the other interviews, however, I felt extremely positive about the Altamonte Springs interview. I actually told MSgt Powers, after the interview, that I was cancelling the two other interviews I had scheduled. He just winked and smiled.

Exactly one week later, Assistant Principal Douglas called me to offer me the job. Of course, I said yes! When it was time to make the move to Altamonte Springs, my family opted out of moving there. My youngest son was a freshman in high school and did not want to up and leave his school and his friends. I was sensitive to this because growing up as a military brat, we moved very often due to my father's Army career. As a teen, I attended three different high schools, and I hated it. Also, due to my wife's Graves' disease treatment, she was under the treatment of a doctor at the world-renowned Moffitt Cancer Center in Tampa. Thus, the timing for them to move to Altamonte Springs was not good.

Not wanting to be separated from my family again, I made the hard choice that I would drive to work every day, there and back to my home in the Tampa area. The distance was roughly 225 miles round trip. The traffic on Interstate 4 between Tampa, Orlando, and Daytona is so congested and compacted at times, it is also known as the I-4 corridor.

My daily routine consisted of getting up at 4:30 a.m. and being on the road by no later than 5:10 a.m. My breakfast consisted of one protein bar, a large cup of coffee, and a bathroom break at the nearly halfway point of Love's Truck Stop, just north of Lakeland. Soon the folks at Love's Truck Stop just started referring to me affectionately as "Sarge."

During the entire school year, I was only late once for the 7:25 a.m. school bell. I always made it there by 7:00 a.m. or before. On that one day I was late, there was a huge accident involving eight cars, the kind that you see on the news with multiple TV station helicopters hovering over. It was at the Osceola County and Polk County line. Emergency vehicles from both counties were on the scene. That morning, due to the massive size of the accident, all lanes going North were closed, and the lanes going South were backed up from the rubberneckers taking a long look at the carnage. I ended up getting to school at about 11:45 a.m. From traveling that stretch of highway at the frequency that I was going, I saw countless results of car accidents. In fact, I witnessed two separate accidents happen in front of me on different days. In one incident, I was able to render minor first aid to a passenger involved. One of my greatest fears was that I would be the one to get into an accident myself because of the sheer amount of time I was on the road to and from school. I was always mindful of this as I rumbled up and down the corridor.

Because of my military background, I seemed to adjust nicely to going back and forth to Altamonte Springs. Mornings got to be bearable because I was able to leave so early, and traffic was not as terrible in the wee hours. Coming back to Tampa, however, was a huge burden. School was released at 2:25 p.m. However, after drill team practice, various other practices, and meetings, I did not leave campus until well after 4:00 p.m.. By that time, I was deep into "rush hour" traffic. I typically walked

New Job – New Challenges

into my home anywhere between 6:30 p.m. and 7:00 p.m.. I did not complain because I loved the school, the kids, my job, and getting to see my family each day. It was worth the drive.

Although I loved teaching AFJROTC at my new school, I noticed a few concerning things about Major Powers and the culture that he had created within the program during his long tenure there. Major Powers had been the senior instructor at LBHS for over 20 years. However, during his active duty military days, he somehow managed to only be stationed at a couple of Air Force bases. Typically, as an officer in the USAF, you will have been assigned to several bases over a 20-year plus career in the USAF, especially as an officer. Although it is not unheard of, it is very unusual. Whenever I asked him about his background in the Air Force, he said he understood how uncommon it was to only be stationed at a couple of bases. He would always say "that's just the hand Uncle Sam dealt me." The lack of assignments was not concerning to me. What was concerning was the fact that he admitted to not having the opportunity to be around and associate with many Blacks, Hispanics, or women during his active duty days of the military.

When President Trump was elected, Major Powers openly said that "Trump was gonna take the country back from the queers, the Black Lives Matter people, Nancy Pelosi, and all the other liberal trash that has infested the country." He said this in front of the cadets as well as me. Although this was not necessarily racist, it gave me a pretty good idea about the senior instructor I was working with.

Major Powers kept a bible on his desk. He would routinely mix bible passages into his lesson plan. He was known to slam his hand down on his bible when he was driving home a point. Even though there is nothing in the JROTC curriculum that actually gives way to the bible, Major Powers somehow drew correlations between the JROTC lesson of the day and the bible. This was a regular occurrence in his class. Major Powers had created this strange cultural mix of Trumpism, low tolerance for others that are different, what some might call "Southern Charm," and a somewhat chauvinistic environment within the JROTC unit. This culture had existed for as long as he had been there and likely before that as well.

Nonetheless, I did not consider Major Powers a racist. I just thought he was ignorant to certain things that pertained to race, ethnicity, and gender. One day during lunch, the Major was watching FOX News on his phone. At the time, former President Trump's lawyer Michael Cohen accused the former president of using the "N" word all the time behind closed doors. Major Powers looked at me and said that he didn't think the "N" word was really that bad. He compared it to the word "Bitch."

"What do you mean, Major?" I asked him.

"When I was growing up, my mom and dad said nigger all the time," he replied casually.

At first, I thought I misheard him. He continued to tell his story and give examples. He told me that one time, back in Mississippi, his mom, dad, he, and his wife were out to dinner. His dad was describing the African-American waiter as a nigger. His wife looked at the Major's father and said, "Would you stop saying nigger."

Although Major Powers was not calling me or anyone else a nigger, just the fact that he said it in front of me three times blew my mind.

New Job – New Challenges

"Major Powers, it's probably not a great idea to just bluntly say the "N" word out in the open like that. You really might offend someone," I told him.

He asked me if I was offended.

"No," I said, "I'm just shocked that you would say the "N" word so nonchalantly."

"Black boys say the word all the time," was his response.

"They say Nigga as a term of endearment, Major. It's a very different scenario than a white man, especially their teacher, saying the word nigger. Very different terms."

I also explained to him that calling the young men in his charge, "black boys," seemed very insensitive. His answer was that all the Politically Correct (PC) stuff was too much for him. He clearly did not get what I was saying. He asked me again if I was offended, and I repeated no. I suggested that he should strongly consider taking a sensitivity class.

"Listen, I'm telling you that President Trump is going to put an end to all of the PC stuff," he answered gruffly and went back to looking at his phone as if the conversation had never happened.

His lack of sensitivity would lead to some African-American students dropping the course as well as a Hispanic student's mother reporting Major Powers to HQ AFJROTC as being a racist after he called her, "a useless waste of oxygen."

CHAPTER 4

A LESSON IN THE LEVELS OF MULTIFACETED DISCRIMINATION

During one of our weekly uniform inspections, I noticed that Major Powers was disciplining one of our cadets. It was unusual for Major Powers to personally discipline a cadet for uniform infractions, as that was the duty of the cadet flight commander. The cadet flight commander is the cadet in charge of their class period and it's their job to implement whatever has been designated by the JROTC Instructors for the day.

When it comes to uniform inspection, our JROTC unit functions very similarly to a college-level ROTC program. Like college-level ROTC, the cadet flight commander and cadet flight sergeant conduct uniform inspections of their flight or class. The instructors typically supervise or watch over the inspection from a distance. Furthermore, it was very rare to see or hear Major Powers yell at a cadet. So, I walked over to see what was happening with Major Powers and the female cadet.

Major Powers was upset because the cadet's hair was not within standards according to the cadet flight commander. He was also involved because the cadet flight commander asked him to intervene on her behalf. As I moved closer, I could hear Major Powers telling the female cadet that she was a disgrace to the JROTC unit. The female cadet began to cry. She tried explaining that she was a cheerleader and that she was going to be cheering later that day at our pep rally, and her hair might be out of regulation because of her involvement in the pep rally. She tried to jog his memory by telling him that she had told him the prior week that her hair would not be in the usual bun and might be touching her collar.

Before she could finish talking, Major Powers told her to shut up. She started crying even harder.

She whimpered, "You let the white girls get away with everything. You never say anything about their hair even when they dye it in all the different shades."

At that point, Major Powers got directly in her face. "Because of students like you, I'm retiring!"

At that point, I stepped in and told Major Powers that I would take it from there. Major Powers walked into the JROTC building and into his office.

I told the cadet to hang in there and to get back in formation. As she walked away to join the other cadets in formation, I noticed that her hair appeared to be within the guidelines of our governing AFJROTC regulation. I called the cadet back over to take a closer look at her hair. I asked her how the situation with Major Powers started.

A Lesson in the Levels of Multifaceted Discrimination

She said that the cadet flight commander deducted points from her because her hair slightly touched the back part of her shirt collar.

"I questioned the cadet flight commander about the red highlights in her own blonde hair," she said.

She said she told the cadet flight commander, who happens to be white, that she was being hypocritical because her red highlights were not natural and were out of regulation. "The cadet flight commander got upset with me and called over Major Powers. She told him that she felt like I was being insubordinate and disrespectful to her."

This black female cadet expressed to me that she was tired of seeing the white female cadets get away with hair infractions and had finally decided to say something.

"You were wrong for being insubordinate to the cadet flight commander. You should have brought it to my attention instead," I told her. "Why didn't you bring this to my attention sooner?

Her answer was that it had always been like that and that I would not be able to change the racist culture of JROTC at Lake Brantley High School. I told her that I would talk to Major Powers about her concerns.

"Good luck," she said, "I'm sorry, but the white female cadets will always get away with things because Major Powers shows them favoritism."

As she got back in formation for the third time, I heard her apologize to the cadet flight commander for being disrespectful. I found her apology to be a significant sign of maturity and leadership from the three-year cadet.

After class, I told Major Powers that the black female cadet was really hurt by the interaction that she had with him. "She feels that you show favoritism towards the white female cadets and let them get away with things," I said.

He looked me in the face and said that she might be right. "I don't understand black females, and I have always been unsure about their hairstyles as it pertains to the United States Air Force, which governs our JROTC appearance standards."

"Maybe you should let me handle the things you're unsure of as it pertains to females' hair standards while in military uniform," I suggested.

He shrugged in agreement and walked away.

At the end of the day, I told the white female cadet flight commander that she would need to fix the red highlights in her hair by the following Wednesday's uniform inspection. She was furious with me and said that she was going to talk to Major Powers about it. "It's never been a problem before," she groused.

"Regulations prohibit red highlights while in military uniform," I explained. "Thus, you are out of regulation until you correct that."

She stormed away. Within 10 minutes of our conversation, according to Major Powers, the cadet flight commander's mother called Major Powers to complain about me telling her daughter that she needed to fix the red highlights by next week's uniform inspection. For the next six days, she kept the

A Lesson in the Levels of Multifaceted Discrimination

red highlights in her hair and made it a point to tell everyone who would listen that she was not getting rid of them.

On that Wednesday, which is uniform inspection day, the red highlights were gone. However, she refused to talk to me the rest of the school year.

The following Monday, the black female cadet's mother came in to speak with Major Powers about the previous incident with her daughter. He referred the mother to me. I told her that her daughter was a great student cadet that embodied exactly what AFJROTC was all about. I did express that her that her daughter was wrong for being disrespectful to the cadet flight commander. However, I also told her that her daughter demonstrated great integrity when she apologized to the cadet flight commander.

"Your daughter would make a great cadet flight commander next year when she's a senior," I told her,

"I doubt my daughter will be returning to JROTC at the end of the school year."

"Why?" I asked.

"I'm sorry, but there are racial overtones within this program. My daughter doesn't need to be subjected to that," she answered.

"JROTC is a great program. I will ensure that every cadet will be treated fairly regardless of their race, ethnicity, gender or sexual orientation," was my reply, and I had every intention of keeping that promise.

I could see the immediate relief on the mother's face as she left my office. Later that evening, I asked Major Powers why he didn't want to talk to the mother, and he said that he was in no mood to deal with an angry black woman. I was very surprised by his frankness and candor. At the time, I just attributed it to him having a long, stressful day but that was not the case.

CHAPTER 5

POPS OF PREJUDICE CRACK THE FOUNDATION

Monday morning seemed to arrive earlier than usual. I thought it just felt that way because I had stayed up late watching the Lakers play basketball. Nonetheless, I pulled myself out of bed and prepared for my regular I-4 commute. I-4 was weird; some days it was busy, other days it was a regular driving experience. On that particular Monday, it was good. It was pleasantly maneuverable with minimal cars on the road.

I arrived at school way ahead of my normal time. I walked into my classroom at about 6:45 a.m. and noted that the Major's stuff was already here. He normally arrived at school at about 5:45 a.m. and would sleep in our logistics supply room till about 7:00 a.m. In the beginning, I thought that it was weird that he slept in there in the morning. However, I got used to this everyday occurrence and just took it in stride as part of his quirky behavior. By this time, it no longer seemed odd. At about 7:15 a.m. he had still not come into the classroom.

I went into logistics, turned on the light and called out, "Major!" He didn't answer, so I walked over to his sleeping bag and nudged him. He was sound asleep and snoring like a freight train. I nudged him again, this time waking him up. He was fully dressed in his military uniform but did not seem to want to be there. I asked him if he was good to go, and he shook his head in the affirmative. This same scenario played out several more times over the next couple of months.

One day, during uniform inspection, he pulled out his lawn chair and sat there as the cadets prepared for inspection. This was a new behavior. Not really alarming, just something that he had not done since I had been there. The cadets thought it was funny, but I thought it was unusual. I asked him if we could talk after school, and he agreed. Later that day, after school, when I walked into the classroom, he was reading the bible while he waited for me. I asked him what scripture he was reading; he replied that he was reading Numbers, Chapter 8 verses 23 -26 of the New International Version.

Not being up to speed on every bible verse, I asked him what it said. He read it word for word.

"The Lord said to Moses, this applies to the Levites: Men twenty-five years old or more shall come to take part in the work at the tent of meeting, but at the age of fifty, they must retire from their regular service and work no longer. They may assist their brothers in performing their duties at the tent of meeting, but they themselves must not do the work. This then, is how you are to assign the responsibilities of the Levites."

He grinned at me as he finished reading.

"Are you one of the Levites?" I asked quickly.

He busted out with a deep belly laugh. Obviously, I was being sarcastic. I knew he meant that he was retiring. He always seemed to find a bible passage for everything he did, so why would his retirement be any different. I asked him if there were any specific reasons as to why he was going to retire.

"This school's changed," was his answer.

"How so?" I asked.

"The kids coming to the school now aren't kids from the local area anymore. They're being bussed in from low-income minority areas, and it's hurting the school.

I asked him in what way. He said that he feared that Lake Brantley High School would soon become a Title 1 school and that he did not want to be around to witness its demise.

"Take a look at how many students are getting free lunch now," he said clearly frustrated by this idea.

For some in academia who like to read the tea leaves and make predictions, the number of kids receiving free lunch may be a sign that Title 1 is on the way. For some, Title 1 classification is looked down upon. I was not privy to the number of kids receiving free lunch at the school, and I am unfortunately not well versed in the different titles. All his explanations and reasoning really didn't matter to me. What I seemed to be hearing was his conviction that the school's racial and class demographics were changing, and it bothered him enough to push him into retirement. He had already demonstrated this point of view when months earlier he yelled at the African-American female about her hair and said it was because of students like her that he would soon retire.

To me, the bible verse that he quoted was just a self-righteous, kinder, and gentler thing to hide behind rather than express his true thoughts. In my opinion, the true reason he was likely retiring is because of the influx of minority kids pouring into the traditionally predominately white school. From this point on, he might have shown up for the job, but emotionally, he had already checked out.

Within weeks, he notified the principal that he would soon be retiring. The principal asked if he would be finishing out the school year, and he declined. With three months left in the school, the Major told me that he was turning all the decision making over to me. He said that he did not want to be involved in the interview process when it was time to hire a new senior instructor. At this point, he was just collecting a paycheck.

Back at the beginning of the school year, Major Powers had installed one of his favorite cadets into the flight sergeant position. Cadet Nobleman was a senior classman and had been in JROTC for all four years. His family were also family friends of the Powers'. He was a really nice kid, but he marched to his own drum, and that drum didn't ever seem to be the Air Force drum. He had a spiked, mullet-styled haircut, dark brown on the sides and bleached blond on the top. He was super popular but none of the cadets took him seriously as a JROTC leader. He was paired up with the JROTC cadet commander. His class was the class with all of the cadet brass and seniors. His class period was our leadership class. He had all the visibility in the unit, so he had major influence. Although he was a great kid, he was not the right cadet to be in a leadership position. I don't think he literally planned it out, but he only wore his uniform every other week. He also had a very low core GPA and was barely maintaining a C in JROTC. Several times I had suggested to the Major that we remove him from such a high-visibility position. Each time, the Major said no.

On the other hand, cadet Alice Vilmer was a sharp, up and coming second-year cadet. She was a straight A student and one of the best marchers in our entire JROTC program. At the time, she did not have a significant role within the unit. However, she volunteered for every special assignment and was the leader of one of our drill teams. She was blunt and business-like in her approach as a student, cadet, and member of the girl's water polo team. She would often complain that Cadet Nobleman was bringing the unit down and that he was a slacker. She would say to me almost on a daily basis that she could do better. Coincidently, she happened to be in the class with Cadet Nobleman and all the other seniors.

The week after Major Powers gave me the authority to run some elements of the unit, I removed cadet Nobleman from the flight sergeant position. He was actually relieved and eager to give up his post. We temporarily put Cadet Vilmer into the flight sergeant position. She took to the position as if she had been doing it for years and never looked back. I was very impressed at how she turned around the attitude of the other cadets. Within weeks, we could see improvement in the unit's marching skills, discipline, and grades. She was not afraid to write up a cadet for poor performance. A couple of times, I had to have her dial back her aggression. However, overall, she was a natural-born leader.

Although we all knew that the Major would soon be retiring, the unit seemed to be sailing along very smoothly. We were getting many opportunities to present and/or post colors at events around the Orlando area. The Orlando Apollos was a professional football team in the new Alliance of American Football coached by football great Steve Spurrier. The owner was a fan of the United States Military. One evening, I decided to go over to his office in downtown Orlando and ask if he would give our color guard a chance to present the colors at their first home game. He was very impressed that I had the audacity to come up to the office in full uniform and ask. He gambled and said yes. After the performance of our "A" Team, an all senior color guard team, the owner was so impressed with how highly trained we were that he asked me if our guys would do all of the Apollo's televised home games. I said yes. It was an awesome accomplishment for our program.

A few weeks later, Major Powers retired, and I was at the helm alone while the hiring process started. Although the Major was gone, we continued to roll. I tried the same approach with the NBA's Orlando Magic that I had taken with the Orlando Apollos. That process was not as simple. Fortunately, the owner of the Apollos was able to get me in with Britany O' Shea of the Magic. One of her many jobs was scheduling talent for the Magic home games. After speaking to her about our color guard team, she was all in.

Our color guard team participation at the Orlando Magic game was truly special. At that time, we had one of the only, if not the only, all-girls JROTC in the area. They were affectionately known as the "Wonder Girls." I gave them that name because individually they had the highest GPA in the unit, the most community service hours, and the most events performed than any of the other cadets. These girls were truly wonder girls, and they were led by Cadet Vilmer. The night of the game, they hung out with the Magic players and were treated like rock stars by the Magic's staff. They crushed the performance and, on that night, the four of them emerged as the future leaders of the unit.

One week prior to the end of school, I solicited applications to fill the positions of the graduating seniors. Most units are run by 4th year cadets with the 3rd year cadets serving as understudies. It doesn't always work out that way. However, at our unit that is what we strived for, as most 4-year cadets will have likely mastered the art of being a complete JROTC cadet—in theory.

Cadet Vilmer applied for the deputy commander position. She said if she could obtain the deputy position it would help her in pursuit of becoming the unit commander in her senior year.

With the help of a few active-duty military recruiters, I reviewed all 50 applications, and I started plugging in names of the cadets for the upcoming school year. Ultimately, Cadet Vilmer was selected to be the deputy corps commander. I had once told Cadet Vilmer and her mother that I had not been blessed with a daughter but if I ever had a daughter that hopefully she would be just like her daughter, Alice. Little did I know at the time that she would be the leader of the effort to drive me out of the school.

CHAPTER 6

A FRESH START TURNS SOUR

The new year started off with a blast. We were rolling with a new senior instructor, a new cadet commander, and Cadet Deputy Commander Vilmer ready to take on the world. It was clear to see on day one that Cadet Vilmer was going to push the cadet commander very hard. He knew this when he applied for the position. Fortunately, they were good friends or at least they had been.

I worked out a deal with the Assistant Principal that the senior cadets could come over to the lounge during lunch and eat together. At first, he was leery of the idea. However, after I explained to him that it was good for the group of leaders to eat together because it would help them gel together as a team and would be a good source of esprit de corps. He agreed but suggested that the instructors would need to monitor them. I agreed.

In year's prior, the JROTC teachers' lounge had been converted into a workspace for the senior cadets to do their JROTC work and reports. This was also the room where they would be allowed to eat together during lunch. It worked perfectly. However, it was also a place where they could be teenagers too, thus, they could get into teenage mischief.

One day, in September 2019, during lunch, I walked in to see what the cadet leaders were up to. There were about 10 or so cadets in the room. One of the top cadets brought in a "wave cap" and suggested that I wear the wave cap to cultivate my "waves." A wave cap is a silky head cap that some African-Americans wear on their heads to help create or cultivate wave in the hair and for keeping hair and hairstyles in place. I sport a shaved head, so he was attempting to ridicule my bald head. All the cadets in the room busted out in a loud roar. They had a running bet to see how I would respond. Although I didn't get offended by it, I didn't find it particularly funny either. I just said, "good one," and walked away.

Two months later, in December 2019, again during lunch, I looked in to check on the cadets as usual. This time, as soon as I walked into the room, one of the leaders said, "Master Sergeant, can you give me permission to say the N-Word?" Again, they all laughed. However, someone yelled out, "You've already said it, so why are you asking for permission?" The room suddenly got awkwardly quiet.

I told the cadet that asked me the question to come with me to the senior instructor's classroom. The senior instructor was not there. So, we sat down, and I asked him what was going on and why he wanted permission to use the "N" word. He responded that it was nothing and asked if he could go just back and join the other cadets. I told him to go ahead. This time I was slightly alarmed, and I decided to write the encounter down in my binder.

A Fresh Start Turns Sour

There seemed to be some defiance circulating within the program. Deputy commander, Cadet Vilmer seemed to be at odds with the cadet commander more and more. Although they were good friends, she was constantly challenging his authority as the program's leader. To use a sports analogy, it was like a divided locker room. The cadet commander was a senior. He was planning on joining the U.S. Navy. He was a great cadet commander and good at calculated reasoning. He had major influence over most of the other seniors in our program, and Cadet Vilmer had major influence over most, if not all, of the underclassmen.

As the instructor, I was expected to officiate and resolve all of their JROTC issues. The new senior instructor deferred from most issues as he had not yet learned much about the cadets and their personalities. Mostly, it was high school drama created by Cadet Vilmer. She often approached situations from an emotional perspective whereas the cadet commander was less emotional. Cadet Vilmer expected me to take her side in every situation. She would argue non-stop and storm away when things did not go her way. When she was angry, she expected all of the underclassmen to be in her corner. She understood that she had major influence over the underclassmen, and she was clearly forcing them to take her side. Her behavior was causing a major riff in the unit between the cadet commander and his loyal seniors and Cadet Vilmer and her gullible underclassmen. The once great friends were not even communicating outside of JROTC. The unit was rapidly deteriorating.

One of the teachers who knew Cadet Vilmer stopped by my classroom one day. She said that she had heard Cadet Vilmer saying how much she hated me. The teacher, who was a good friend of mine, asked Cadet Vilmer why she was so upset with MSgt Hopkins. Cadet Vilmer said that I never took her side and that I always took the side of the cadet commander. She said she wished that I would be replaced with someone that was more in line with her point of view as the cadet deputy commander. This teacher asked Cadet Vilmer if she had any examples to demonstrate how she came to have this point of view. Cadet Vilmer stated that she wanted more autonomy, more authority, and less leadership activity from the instructors. She wanted to decide what days uniform inspections were held on, she wanted to help decide what subjects were taught by the instructors, and she wanted to decide what the punishment would be when a cadet got into trouble. She kept referencing how JROTC is "cadet run." The teacher suggested that maybe Cadet Vilmer was looking at "cadet run" through a skewed literal lens. "Yes, it is cadet run but, instructor driven, and instructor guided, like a coach coaching a team," she told her. "Those kinds of requests sound like curricular adjustments, which according to the school district, would need to be handled by the instructors and the principal of the school, not a student," she continued.

Even the teacher thought that this was a bit too much to for a student to ask for. Nonetheless, Cadet Vilmer was not able to understand the concept. She seemed to be forgetting that she was in a high school program and not a dictatorship. I had seen this sort of attitude many times before while teaching high school JROTC, but never to this extent. Power and influence can be hard to manage for adults at times. For teenagers, having power and influence can be a recipe for disaster. As an instructor and mentor in a structured program like JROTC you have to say no sometimes, but with an explanation especially when it comes to the JROTC curriculum. For Cadet Vilmer, hearing me tell her no was not the option that she wanted to hear.

Cadet Vilmer once asked if she could recommend a cadet get a failure on his uniform inspection.

"Why would you want to fail the cadet?" I asked her.

"To each him a lesson," was her answer.

"I am not able or willing to fail a student merely to teach him a lesson," I replied.

"In my opinion, your reasoning is weak," she replied curtly.

"Cadet, this is real life, and tampering with a student's GPA just to teach them a lesson is unethical. If you were a teacher, how would you explain to the kid's parents that you gave their child an F just to teach him a lesson? Don't you think that those parents would have good reason to be upset?"

Cadet Vilmer did not like that I did not agree with her, and she stormed off. To me, that entire situation was full of emotions on the part of Cadet Vilmer.

About a week or so later, during lunch on January 15, 2020, I was sitting at my desk talking to another teacher when Cadet Vilmer and two other underclassmen cadets entered my classroom. While the other teacher and I talked, she was also playing music from YouTube on her phone. As if rehearsed, the three cadets collectively asked the teacher to play the Cotton-Eyed Joe song and chided me to teach them how to do the Cotton-Eyed Joe dance. Unbeknownst to the teacher, they were using her as part of their set-up. As the teacher played the Cotton-Eyed Joe song on YouTube, the three cadets crowded around my desk and began to jump around in front of me kicking their feet together and saying heehaw. They all joined in, encouraging me to join in with them and teach them how to do the dance.

To diffuse the situation and get rid of the three cadets, I told them to go get the senior instructor and have him do the dance instead of me. I did not think that they would go and get him. Sure enough, he entered my classroom and started half-heartedly dancing around as the cadets followed him into my classroom. As the Cotton-Eyed Joe song played on the teacher's phone, I became furious at both the cadets as well as the senior instructor. The senior instructor zoomed out of my classroom quickly. Obviously, he began to realize that they were using him as well, and he hadn't realized what they were up to. The teacher playing the music was in no way involved in the shenanigans. She was just manipulated by Cadet Vilmer and the two other cadets. When it was all said and done, the teacher looked at me and said, "What the hell just happened?"

She was appalled and felt used by the cadets. She is Caucasian and stated to me that she was shocked by the whole episode and that they would have never done that to her as a white person. It was such an odd episode that she suggested that I document the incident.

January 15, 2020 would prove to be a trying and eventful day as major racial tensions were about to quickly explode.

CHAPTER 7

HATEFUL ALT RIGHT WORDS SPEWED ON INSTAGRAM AND IN PRINT

Someone once said when it rains it pours; if true, January 2020, at Lake Brantley High School, would prove to be a monsoon.

Still reeling from the Cotton-Eyed Joe incident during lunchtime, my class later that same day brought more disturbing events. During sixth period, my deputy flight commander, Cadet Nichols approached me. She was very distraught.

"Master Sergeant, how could you do this to me?" she asked somberly.

"What are you talking about?" I asked.

She pulled out her phone and showed me what appeared to be an Instagram account with my school picture as its avatar. The name on the account was realbrantleyrotcmemes. I was completely blindsided.

She pointed to a post and sadly said, "Why would you say this horrible thing about me, MSgt?"

"Cadet Nichols, you know me, I would never make fun of a cadet. That is not what I'm about," I responded.

"I know Master Sergeant, but the account looks real," she responded, calmly.

I felt very bad for Cadet Nichols. It seemed that the creator of the account was using me to bully her. I realized that whoever created the account had been the one to post the derogatory garbage about Cadet Nichols, and it was starting to gain likes from several members of our JROTC unit. To my surprise, the cadets were liking the post using their actual Instagram pages with their actual pictures of themselves as their avatars for the whole world to see. They had all started following the account on the same day the "realbrantleyrotcmemes" account was created. Either it was a huge coincidence, or the cadets knew of its creation from the individual who created it.

As a parent myself, I knew that I needed to contact Cadet Nichols's parents ASAP to let them know that I did not create the "realbrantleyrotcmemes" account and that I did not and would never make fun of their daughter or any other student. First, I needed to get my leadership involved. As soon as the bell rang, I took Cadet Nichols with her phone directly to the principal's office. I set the phone on his desk and gave him the opportunity to decipher what he was looking at. He immediately sent me to report the incident to the school's resource officer.

Because it involved a student, and a serious accusation lobbied against me, I decided to inform the school district's superintendent via email as well, just as a precaution in case my school principal didn't feel the incident qualified as important enough to notify the superintendent. I figured that as the superintendent of schools, he could do whatever he wanted to with the information and should be informed of the incident.

At the end of the school day, I called Cadet Nichols's mother to warn her of the "realbrantleyrotcmemes" Instagram account. To my surprise, she had already seen the post.

"Mrs. Nichols, I am so sorry that your daughter had to endure this treatment," I said. "I just want to assure you that I did not create the 'realbrantleyrotcmemes' page, and I did not say what it appears I said."

"Master Sergeant, I am not mad or upset. I just thought you were a teacher that likes to have fun with his students," she replied.

"Yes, ma'am, I enjoy teaching. However, I would never do anything on the level of bullying a student or making fun of them."

I was surprised but grateful that she took the position of not being too bothered by the incident. I assumed that she would be furious. Nonetheless, I was furious that this had occurred. I knew that if it had gone the other way, meaning that if Cadet Nichols' mother had initiated a complaint to the school about me and the post, I would have been left to defend myself and possibly been out of a job. There would have been no way I would have been able to uncover who created the "realbrantleyrotcmemes" page and who made the post without employing the help of an attorney and/or a private investigator. Thus, I wanted to be proactive.

That night I went home and tried to put everything in perspective. I was trying to put my arms around everything that had transpired during the day. It was a lot to handle, but I felt, at this point, it all seemed as though it might still be manageable. My naivete allowed me to think that it was just some kids being mischievous. I did not think that this was a full-on assault of me as a JROTC instructor. As I thought about it a while longer, I kept asking myself if the culprits were hoping that Cadet Nichols's mother would have taken a tougher stance and come after me by contacting the school to complain. At this point, I had no reason to believe that this was the case.

Sometime later, after I had already left Lake Brantley High School, through another cadet, I found out that this was indeed the case. Because Cadet Nichols' mother was known to be a quick-tempered, fiery parent, she was expected by the renegade cadets to take the bait and contact the school in disgust and anger to have me fired. However, for some reason, Mrs. Nichols did not behave as they had expected.

The next morning, I rolled into school guarded and somewhat suspicious of all our cadets. I assumed the worst had passed, but I was still on guard. As first period zoomed by, and we rolled into 2nd period, Cadet O'Connor approached me with a serious look on her face. She had her phone out.

"Master Sergeant, I gotta show you something important."

"What is it cadet O'Conner?" I asked.

"I have to show you some serious Instagram stuff."

I smiled and told her that I had already seen the fake Instagram page the day prior.

"No! This is different, it's about you specifically, sir," she answered.

Hateful Alt Right Words Spewed on Instagram and in Print

I looked at her phone. At first, it just appeared to be a few cadets led by Cadet Vilmer ranting and complaining about wanting to have more control over the unit. Nothing that I had not already heard. As I read on, the whole scope changed. By the fourth or fifth page of text messages, I saw my name. I read things such as NIGGER, NIGGEEEEER, MSgt needs to be "tarred and feather" (which I had to actually look up because I had never heard the phrase before) and "No niggers in my corps."

I suddenly felt empty and completely blindsided. Still recovering from the Instagram activities from the day before, I was stunned at the utter vitriol of the language being used about me. The dialog showed that Cadet Vilmer was leading a somewhat loosely concerted effort to drive me out of the JROTC program at Lake Brantley High School. They had discussed several scenarios and situations. For example, if MSgt Hopkins does this, I'll do such and such. If he says this, then we'll do such and such and so on. All the routine high school drama that I had grown accustomed to suddenly got serious. For the second time in two days, I found myself reporting a racially motivated incident to the principal and the school district's superintendent. This time I reported all the activity to HQ AFJROTC as well via email.

That night, I found myself again trying to figure out exactly what was happening. It all seemed like a cluster fuck. Being in the military for 23 years, I was accustomed to the use of foul language. I have used my fair share of choice words over my military career. However, when I retired from the military in 2013, I made myself a promise that I would not use that sort of language around my then 8-year-old son and my teenage son. I basically removed all foul language from my vocabulary. That promise went out the window at the dinner table that night in 2020.

NO NIGGERS IN MY CORPS

I had been keeping what happened to me from my family until I could get a better understanding of what was going on. I decided to tell them what I was dealing with at school as they could tell that I was noticeably stressed. As I described what had happened over the past two days, I blurted out, "What the fuck is going on with these privileged-assed JROTC kids at Lake Brantley High School?!"

That's when I realized that things were getting out of control in my life as a JROTC instructor at this school. At the time, I didn't think the cadets were capable of much more of this type of viscous behavior. However, I knew that if something else did occur, I would need strong support from either my Air Force leadership or my school leadership or both, depending on the severity of the situation.

***

A few days went by since the first incident had happened. There was still tension in the air, and things were still in motion as far as finding out which cadets had contributed to the incidents and what punishments were going to be handed out. Nonetheless, I was hoping for the best as it pertained to support from the school district and the Air Force JROTC folks.

As I drove up I-4 on my way to school, I decided to listen to the "I Have a Dream" speech by Martin Luther King, Jr. I found it ironic that my situation had played out during Mr. King's birthday week. I wondered if my situation was a coincidence or a planned attack by Cadet Vilmer and her band of followers. When I heard Mr. King say, "let us not wallow in the valley of despair," I was instantly uplifted. I felt a strong sense of belief that this issue with these racists cadets would work itself out. After listening to Mr. King's entire speech, I arrived at school feeling refreshed and in a positive mindset. It was Tuesday, January 21, 2020, and I was going to be teaching about World War II, which was one of my favorite subjects to teach, so I was very excited about it.

As I was discussing the war during second period, the flight commander ran into the classroom. "MSgt come into the hallway fast!" she yelled.

"Is there someone hurt," I exclaimed.

"No, there's a huge sign on your door."

I thought she was pranking me, but I could see by the look on her face that she was dead serious. She frantically pointed to the sign. Someone had put a huge sign on my door that read 'Blood and Soil.'

One of the cadets told me that it was a reference to Charlottesville and the Alt Right Movement. This incident, along with the sign, was reported by the senior instructor directly to one of the assistant principals. I finished out the day, but I decided to take some time off from school. I took the next three days off in conjunction with the weekend. I needed to use the time off to do some serious soul searching.

CHAPTER 8

EXPECTED VS ACTUAL RESPONSE

Monday rolled around. As I drove into the school parking lot, I remember thinking how it was sunny and unseasonably warm for February. As I parked my car, I suddenly saw the school through a different lens. Although it was a warm and humid morning, the school suddenly felt cold.

I walked down the long corridor that runs between the two main buildings towards the JROTC building like I always did. But today, I wasn't thinking about my lesson plans or assignments for my students. Instead, I wondered if one of the cadets might key my car and leave a long, ugly scratch on it or if my classroom was going to be somehow tampered with. Would there be more signs or something worse? I felt like a foreigner in the school. I had the thought, why I am here? I kept asking myself, is it worth it? For the first time in my career, I had doubts. I wondered if I could effectively teach at a high level that day ... or any day at this school, with these students.

These questions would rage on for the next couple of days. One of my students even told me that he felt sorry for me and that I looked tired and pitiful. I did not want pity from a student. I wanted to be an effective JROTC instructor, but I was struggling with just being at the school.

Obviously, I was hurt by the actions of some of the cadets that I had guided and mentored. Like many other JROTC instructors, I had put in the time and effort to help mold our cadets into citizens of character and develop their self-discipline, so, yes, I was disappointed and shocked by their actions and behavior. On the other hand, I was beyond disappointed in the school's leadership. I was pissed off and disgusted with the lack of support from the Lake Brantley principal and Seminole County School District. No immediate action had been taken despite everything that had happened. There was no plan of action to remediate the situation and bring the students who were creating this situation to task. It was as if they were moving in slow motion about something that was happening to me at full speed.

I had read several stories of similar racist situations that happened around the United States in other high schools. Most principals were outfront with fair to strong leadership. At a minimum, they all had one thing in common. They all addressed their respective high school students either over the intercom or in the auditorium. Although their speeches varied, some showed emotion and some were blunt and straight to the point, their message seemed to be the same. Racist incidents will not go unpunished in this school! Obviously, they delivered the message in their own style, peppered with different antidotes and phrases. It seemed that nipping things in the bud was what principals were trained to do.

Expected vs Actual Response

That was not the case at Lake Brantley High School. During the entire ordeal, not one time did the principal even come down to the JROTC section to speak with me or make an appearance. As a matter of fact, the principal never addressed this massive racial issue with the school's student population or with his teachers.

On February 5, 2020, I notified the principal, via letter, that I was resigning at the end of that school day. I reminded him that there were several racist incidents directed towards me and that they had not been addressed or corrected. On several occasions, I was tormented, ridiculed, and humiliated by cadets in my school's JROTC program. In my opinion, the school's response was neither timely nor sufficient in adequately addressing the incidents.

As a father, I feel strongly about teachable moments. Teachable moments are extremely valuable because sometimes teens make mistakes. Sometimes these are painful mistakes. These mistakes are opportunities for us as educators and parents to help our children more deeply understand our values. These are the moments when our values go from being mere words we speak, to actions that we take.

I had reported all of the major incidents to the principal and his team as is typical protocol for such incidents. For whatever reason, he and his team refused to take the opportunity to talk to "ALL" of the cadets involved in "ALL" of the hateful incidents directed towards me. On February 5, in speaking with a couple of the cadets that I knew were involved, they informed me that they had not be spoken to or chastised at all.

This was twenty-two days after I had reported the first incident.

NO NIGGERS IN MY CORPS

The Air Force took a stronger stance. The director of AFJROTC at the time, Colonel Sanders, was very supportive. He could not do much as far as discipline and investigation of the incidents because it was under the jurisdiction of the school and the school district. Although there are over a thousand Air Force JROTC instructors worldwide and well over 120,000 students in AFJROTC, Colonel Sanders still found time to call me several times to see how things were going with the school and their investigation. He told me that I had his support to transfer to any school that was available. He also "slammed" the senior instructor as well as the school to nip the whole thing in the bud. He told me that he was born and raised in the deep South, and he knew how hurtful the "N" word could be and the history behind it. Colonel Sanders, however, was also retiring soon from the United States Air Force and was not able to do much to influence the Seminole County School District and Lake Brantley High School.

During the runup to my resignation, I spoke to several other high school principals that I knew. They all said something similar: When the hateful and racists incidents occurred, the principal should have quickly and strongly denounced the racist acts in clear, unambiguous terms to the entire school, or at a minimum the entire JROTC unit. His silence and minimal response to all the hateful and racist acts perpetrated against me allowed for misinformation, confusion, fear, and distrust to grow. Personally, I believe that due to the principal's lackluster response in effectively addressing the situation, he allowed for a racially hostile environment to exist in his school as if it was condoned.

According to the Seminole County Public School (SCPS) Code:

Expected vs Actual Response

> "Every employee, student, or applicant for employment at SCPS has a solemn right to be treated fairly, equally, equitably, and with dignity. It is the policy of the School Board of Seminole County, Florida, that no employee, student, or applicant shall—on the basis of race, color, national origin, sex, disability, marital status, age, religion, or any other basis prohibited by law—be excluded from participating in, be denied the benefits of, or be subjected to discrimination and harassment under any educational programs, activities or in any employment conditions, policies, or practices conducted by the district."

Based on these SCPS statements, the racist incidents I endured, and the principal's silence and minimal response, made clear that I was not treated fairly, equally, equitably, or with dignity.

I served the country in the Air Force for 23 years, and I was never called a Nigger or never even racially insulted by my fellow military service members. As a AFJROTC instructor at Lake Brantley High School, I was under constant fear that the racists and hateful attacks would continue, so I resigned from my position as an Air Force JROTC Instructor at Lake Brantley High School. As I stated in my resignation letter, the actions of a handful of cadets demonstrated very little respect for me as a retired Air Force veteran and JROTC Instructor. Most importantly, their actions showed little respect for me as a human being.

The principal's outright refusal to swiftly address the student body about the racial incidents in my classroom or at a minimum, his refusal to address the JROTC students' Instagram hate speech gave way to the incident where the "Blood and Soil" sign was left on my classroom door. These students, still under his principalship, were allowed to continue to ramp up their racist activities. How much further would they take this knowing that no disciplinary actions were coming their way?

I didn't want to stick around to find out.

It's likely that if the principal and SCPS would have taken swift, strong, and appropriate actions, the harassment would have ceased, and the "Blood and Soil" sign would likely have never been placed on my classroom door. Any reasonable human being would have resigned as well under these trying circumstances.

SCPS also stated that the principal felt that I was satisfied with the results of the investigation. I did not express satisfaction with the results of the investigation nor was I ever asked if I was satisfied with the results of the investigation.

The senior JROTC instructor at Lake Brantley chose to meet with the principal while I was taking time away to clear my head. He did this on his own, without telling me when he was going to meet with the administration. In the beginning of the discovery of the social media attacks, I met with the principal to show him the Instagram texts. However, I had also planned to meet with him to discuss the outcome of everything, but the senior instructor took it upon himself to meet with principal on my behalf to "smooth everything over." I was furious because he had no authority to speak for me.

Seminole County Public Schools is a large organization with the resources and the know-how to make real and true change in a young person's life if they choose to do so. In my situation, they decided not to use their influence, power, and resources to change the behavior and/or mindset of the students involved in the racist attacks on me.

Expected vs Actual Response

I resigned from my position and walked away from a good, well-paid teaching job. Unfortunately, the fear of more incidents and lack of support from my administration led to my "Constructive Dismissal." The perpetration of these racist attacks on me by some of my cadets and the nonchalant and unconcerned approach by the school's principal and SCPS toward the incidents was unacceptable.

The entire situation demonstrated very little respect for me as an Air Force veteran and a JROTC Instructor. Most importantly, these actions, in totality, showed little respect for me as a human being. I became an educator to make a positive impact in young people's lives, not to be treated less than human by a bunch of privileged, racist students. As a matter of proper business, and to get the incidents on record, I filed a complaint in March 2020 with the United States Equal Employment Opportunity Commission (EEOC). After a thorough investigation, the EEOC confirmed that my case (511-2020-02149) reached the threshold to allow me to file a federal lawsuit against the school district, and they delivered me the "Right to Sue" notice.

I did not file a lawsuit. I plan on moving on with my life. However, it seems that every day these hateful stories keep happening around the country, and it feels like it's only getting worse.

In the following weeks, I received an anonymous text from someone telling me that they were happy that me and my story had made it to the "chimpout.org" website because that's all that I was worth.

CHAPTER 9

OUTRAGE AND SUPPORT

These days, it seems that when the civil rights generation hears of racial injustice, it garners an instinct to rally in support of the person or persons being attacked. My parents are no different. Although they are extremely patriotic, they are still members of the civil rights generation. My mother's point of view is especially colorful.

Before I go into my mother's outrage at the racial incidents, let me tell you a little bit about my mother. First of all, my mother is an "Army Wife." Because most of the time, dad was either out in the field practicing for war or deployed somewhere around the world, like most army wives, she had to be dad, enforcer, bill payer, homework helper, dinner maker, and just about everything else. In addition, she is an ordained Southern Baptist minister. She is used to operating in a male-dominated world and can verbally go toe-to-toe with the best of them.

She doesn't like conflict.

However, she never backs down from it either, especially if it involves one of her children. One will get a healthy dose of her Southern wit, her expertise on life, and the Bible if she's forced to go there. However, she is the sweetest person that you will ever meet and a world-class listener.

Back in 2004, while I was on active duty, I was sent on temporary duty to the Port Mortuary at Dover Air Force Base in Delaware. The port mortuary in Dover is where all Americans are returned if they lose their life in battle or conflict outside the United States. The United States Marines were about to push into Fallujah, Iraq as part of Operation Iraqi Freedom and Operation Enduring Freedom. As a result, the United States was expecting heavy casualties. I was part of the three-man dental forensics team tasked with taking full-mouth x-rays on the deceased heroes. During my team's assignment at the mortuary, we performed full mouth x-rays on 107 of these heroes.

Every single night, for the entire duration of our mission, my wonderful mother called me and just listened. She did not say much unless I asked a question. She mostly prayed ... and listened. She knew that I was not good when having to deal with death. Thus, she became my instant psychologist on duty every night. As my weight dwindled down from 200 lbs. to 170 lbs., mom was there on the other end of the phone trying to help me get my appetite back and keep up my focus and mental health. Many people lost weight and had no appetite because the charred remains of the deceased heroes looked like BBQ. The texture of the remains looked like burnt meat. It was hard to look at my actual food the same way after seeing, touching, and handling the horrific remains we were tasked to work on day after day.

Within the first two weeks of our tour of duty, we lost our active-duty psychologist due to mental fatigue. The ever-present smell of formaldehyde in her clothing and hair, as well as the amount of counseling that she was doing by herself became too much for her.

There were seven steps or stations in the identification process. Our psychologist was the sole counselor of this mission and the various teams. I had never taken x-rays on a deceased person, let alone a beheaded person. We took x-rays on several Americans that had been beheaded by the Iraqis. It was a very sad experience, and it began to take its toll on us all.

However, my mother was there with me every night. She helped me understand that these men and women had given the ultimate sacrifice to their country, and it was now my job to make sure that they were returned to their families with dignity and respect. My mother's humility and civility were on full display as she nurtured her son's mental health via telephone.

Now that you have had a chance to see mom's softer side, let me tell you about her reaction when I told her about what happened at Lake Brantley High School. Immediately, she went into momma bear mode.

"I'm coming down there to Florida to deal with this school," she said.

"Mom," I said, "I've got this under control. I'm a grown military man, I think I'll be okay."

"Who changed your dirty diapers when you were a baby?" she exclaimed. "I'll be on the next plane to Altamonte. I'm going to give them all a piece of my mind. First, I'm going to talk to that bible- thumping Major that bred this racist culture. Then, I'm calling the school board, the superintendent, and the principal," she exclaimed, as her voice rose to a higher pitch. "They don't know me like that," she rattled. I'm an Army wife. I'm built for this type of stuff."

"Mom, I get it, you're pissed; I am too," I said, smiling as I realized the love she was pouring out for me.

Even though she was being sarcastic to a point, I knew that she was just showing concern for her first-born child. She knew that I would do the best that I could under the circumstances. She would come if I needed her, but she trusted me to do the right thing and that meant everything to me.

Dad, on the other hand was cool and calculated. He always preaches about harnessing one's anger to use it as positive energy. His approach to my situation was strategic and militaristic. He told me that I needed to hit back in a two-pronged attack.

"First, document everything," he said.

I replied, "Check," in agreement.

"Make a note of all the parties involved in leadership and what their responsibilities are," he said. "Challenge them on paper and strike with pinpoint accuracy. Cut off their ability to strike first and prepare for any retaliation."

The calmness in his voice as he laid out my strategy was almost chilling. "Surprise attack, son, and then fight to win the war not the battle," he said. "Hit them hard when they least expect it."

Pop's advice would prove to be spot on, as writing this book is my way of channeling my anger and frustration with the racial attacks and lackluster support from the school into something positive by allowing me to tell my story.

Support at any level is always great. It's particularly awesome when the support comes from those who are not on one's radar. That unknown support came in the form of a veteran's group called Justice4vetsNow. Unbeknownst to me, Justice4vetsNow found out about what happened to me, and they started a huge support blitz on my behalf. First, they contacted the Orlando News station, Channel 9. Then, they contacted headquarters, the EEOC in Washington, D.C. who directed the Florida office to contact me directly.

I have no idea how the EEOC got my mobile phone number, but they called me. All they said was that they had been directed by the D.C. headquarters to reach out to me. To this day, I have not been able to track down Justice4vetsNow to say thank you. I was told that their mission is to fight for vets when vets can't fight for themselves. I wish that I could show them my gratitude for watching my six! I'll keep looking. Maybe one day I'll figure out who they are. Somehow, I think they know that I am grateful for their support. My gut tells me that secrecy is their strength.

A team color guard: LBHS JROTC MSGT Hopkins and Steve Spurrier

My first classroom at Ashley Ridge

Father and Son in uniform

Wonder Girls: LBHS Color Guard

Pop just back from Vietnam 1969-1970

Pop just before Army retirement

Thank You
Master Sergeant Anthony Hopkins

L B H S   2 0 1 9

I chose to recognize Master-Sergeant Hopkins because of the way he has affected me and my time in JROTC. Even though I have only known him this year I immediately saw the impact he had on me and everyone around him, spreading his positive attitude and words of wisdom. Master-sergeant Hopkins has helped me grow tremendously as a leader, student, and most of has made me a better person.

Travis Williamson
Cum Laude
Lake Brantley High School

"I chose to recognize Master-Sergeant Hopkins because of the way he has affected me and my time in JROTC. Even though I have only known him this year, I immediately saw the impact he had on me and everyone around him, spreading his positive attitude and words of wisdom. Master-sergeant Hopkins has helped be grow tremendously as a leader, student, and most of has made me a better person."

—TRAVIS WILLIAMSON

Thank You
Master Sergeant Anthony Hopkins

L B H S   2 0 1 9

Master Sargent Hopkins, who had taught me in my JROTC class, was a vital figure for me this year. He is an outstanding teacher who cared about my well-being. We had laughs together and had many insightful conversations about aviation, the military and different wars in history. His class is my favorite out of all the ones I attended, I love attending the JROTC and consider it to be the best part of high school. Anthony Hopkins is more than a good teacher, he is a good friend and a figure I look up to.

Jasper Ede
Summa Cum Laude
Lake Brantley High School

"Master Sargent Hopkins, who had taught me in my JROTC class, was a vital figure for me this year. He is an outstanding teacher who cared about my well-being. We had laughs together and had many insightful conversations about aviation, the military and different wars in history. His class is my favorite out of all the ones I attended. I love attending the JROTC and consider it to be the best part of high school. Anthony Hopkins is more than a good teacher, he is a good friend and a figure I look up to."

—JAPSER EDE

Mansion at Magnolia Plantation

Menacing oak tree and slave cabin at Magnolia Plantation

CHAPTER 10

RESOLUTION

I never thought about joining the JROTC while I was in high school. Because my father was in the Army, we moved about every three or four years. Thus, I attended three different high schools. I would see the Jay-ROT-Cee kids in their uniforms, but they seemed too rigid and too square for me. The discipline that they demonstrated was too military-like for my taste at the time. I was never, ever going to join the military. Just like I was never going to get married, and I was never ever going to have any kids. Obviously, like many other teenagers, I had no clue what the journey of life had charted for me.

It was more than 40 years ago when I first encountered a JROTC kid. I was in the 9th grade, and the cadet in question was a senior. Our fathers were stationed in Nürnberg (Nuremberg), Germany, and we attended Nurnberg American High School. This kid was super sharp in his JROTC uniform. It seemed like he had more shiny objects on his uniform than General Patton ever had. I asked the cadet if he was going to join the Army.

"No, not necessarily," he replied.

"Why do you look like that then, bro?" I asked.

"Look like what?" He responded.

As he smiled. I snapped back at him, "You look like some type of General from a third-world country."

We both cracked up laughing, and he came clean with me that he was using JROTC to assist him correct his behavioral issues and to help him prepare for life after high school. This could include the military if he chose that route. This kid, Paul, seemed to be onto something. He was taking advantage of JROTC as a foundation for life.

When I retired from the Air Force in 2013, I was at a job fair for veterans in Tampa. As I walked around from table to table, I noticed a face that looked familiar behind one of the tables. As I made my way over to this man, I kept thinking to myself that the guy looked very familiar.

In the military, everyone's name is on their military uniform. So, over a 23-year time period, I learned that if I forgot someone's name, I would just take a peek at their military nametag on their shirt, and I would be good to go. This came in very handy many times while in service. However, it's made me not so good at remembering people's names. But, I never forget a face. Unfortunately, placing someone's face can be a challenge when you've met lots of people. I walked up to the table, and he greeted me pleasantly. As he began pitching his company to me, I had flashbacks of one of my several high schools. I interrupted him midway into his pitch.

"Sir, you look very familiar to me," I exclaimed.

"I was thinking the same thing," he replied clearly excited.

He asked if I was ever employed by his company, to which I replied, no. After 15 minutes or so of the back and forth and were you ever here or worked there sort of banter, we figured it out. The guy behind the table was the JROTC kid from Nurnberg American High School. Small world! As we reminisced, he told me that he did four years in the Army, which paid for his bachelor's degree. After fulfilling his commitment to the Army and receiving an honorable discharge, he continued his education. The G.I. Bill paid for his master's degree. Over time, Paul rose to become the regional director of Human Resourses, covering 12 East Coast states. He attributed his success to his JROTC foundation.

Today, AFJROTC is still a great foundation builder for life. In some ways, today's AFJROTC is even better because of the great scholarship opportunities and flight-training opportunities it provides. In some cases, cadets are earning more flying hours than they are driving regular motor vehicle hours. AFJROTC is an outstanding program. Its curriculum is tried and true. Although most schools classify JROTC as an elective, JROTC is truly a program. There are about 870 AFJROTC units around the world and over 125,000 students enrolled in the program.

Although this is the chapter designated as the "resolution" chapter, I'd like to spend a bit of time discussing just how great the AFJROTC program is. At its core, AFJROTC objectives are simple and clear. In doing so, its mission is to develop citizens of character dedicated to serving their nation and community. The goal is to educate high school cadets in citizenship and education. The program goals are to instill values of citizenship, service to the United States, personal responsibility, and a sense of accomplishment.

A student who completes two years of Air Force JROTC can enlist in the USAF and receive one stripe or the rank of Airman. Additionally, a student that completes three years of AFJROTC can enlist in the Air Force and receive two stripes or the rank of Airman First Class. As the Air Force website states, cadets who choose to go on to college may receive Air Force ROTC scholarships. As I have witnessed, many of the scholarships end up paying two, three, or four years of tuition, fees, and books.

According to the AFJROTC home page, the curriculum is comprised of leadership education (40 %), aerospace science (40 %), and health and wellness studies (20 %). As you can see, the program is outstanding and is very well laid out. If there is an internal problem with a school's program, it normally stems from the personal beliefs of the Senior Aerospace Science Instructor (SASI) or the Aerospace Science Instructor (ASI) and not the curriculum or standards of AFJROTC itself.

With nearly 1,900 retired officers and enlisted individuals teaching AFJROTC, there is great opportunity for an instructor's influence on a cadet. This influence can be personal beliefs, personal experiences, and/or their upbringing. These influences often seep into the program as well. Here lies the strength of the program and in some cases, the weakness of the program. For a long, tenured instructor who has been at the same high school for many years, there is likely a culture that's been created by the instructor(s). This culture might be good and healthy. However, in some cases, a program unfortunately may contain racist, sexist, homophobic, or other elements that are not conducive to building character in young adults. In my opinion, such was the case with the Lake Brantley High School JROTC program. The SASI had been there for over 20 years. He had racist tendencies. As a result, these racist tendencies created a racist culture. This racist culture went unchecked for many years until my arrival. One would have to be naive to assume that this only existed at the Lake Brantley JROTC program. Although, within any school, there are likely racists amongst the staff, the USAF prides itself on doing the right thing all the time. Thus, racist or derogatory behavior is unacceptable by active-duty members as well as retired Air Force instructors.

So, how do you fix it? Some instructors may say that it does not need to be fixed, or there is nothing to fix. On the contrary, just google racism in JROTC, and you will come across many fixable opportunities. In my opinion, the Director of the Air Force Junior ROTC needs to get out and visit more high school JROTC programs. Although the director sends out a representative to inspect each program every two or three years, the director does not personally get out and visit many schools around the country. When the director's representative comes to a high school for a scheduled inspection, that representative is typically spending most of his or her time with the cadet leadership. This is not the problem. In my opinion, the director needs to have more short-notice visits to more schools. Principals and Assistant Principals conduct visits and evaluations with JROTC instructors all the time. Why shouldn't the Director of the Air Force Junior ROTC make visits as well? Some school AFJROTC programs are not performing up to standards. Headquarters knows which schools are having troubles. Why not send the director to some of these schools?

The Director of the Air Force Junior ROTC is not that far removed from any AFJROTC program. When my story broke in reference to Lake Brantley's JROTC, the Director of the Air Force Junior ROTC at the time called me directly on two occasions to extend his support. Thus, it is not that difficult to speak to one of the 1,900 AFJROTC instructors.

Our curriculum is written by HQAFJROTC, not by the school districts around the country. Therefore, any changes or additions are approved by the Director of the Air Force Junior ROTC and can be placed into production by HQJROTC.

When I first started teaching AFJROTC, I had a conversation with another instructor about drug abuse amongst high school students around the country. To my surprise, there was a chapter in one of our AFJROTC school books that covers drug and alcohol abuse. It is a subject that we teach in JROTC. I was so impressed that we were addressing the issues of drug and alcohol abuse in AFJROTC. I was pleasantly surprised when I found out that in the (40 %) segment of our leadership education portion of AFJROTC, not only do we teach chapters covering Substance Abuse, but we also teach chapters covering:

- Ethics, Values, and Morals
- Attitude, Discipline and Respect
- Note Taking and Study Skills
- Managing Stress
- Making Positive Decisions
- Avoiding and Preventing Violence
- Medicines and Drugs
- Understanding Your Body Image

My point is that everything that we teach and all our AFJROTC specific curriculum activity is approved by the Director of the Air Force Junior ROTC personally.

I also had a conversation with another instructor who was not happy that two of his cadets were involved in a same-sex relationship outside of JROTC. He told me that he had a problem with it. It was during a drill meet in Daytona Beach. I commented on how well the two cadets were performing their drill movements. The instructor flat out told me that they were gay. He said that he had been trying to figure out how to get them out of AFJROTC because it was affecting the morale of the unit.

I said, "Bro, this ain't the military, these are high school kids. If it's a PDA thing, then enforce the PDA rules across the board. However, if it's just because YOU have a problem with homosexuality, that's your personal prerogative. But trying to figure out how to kick the two cadets out of the JROTC program over their sexuality just doesn't feel right."

He just smirked and walked away. In my opinion, that was that instructor's personal belief. However, his stupidity has likely been seeping into a great program and causing the unit's morale to drop. How do you fix that? It obviously takes time. However, if the Director of the Air Force Junior ROTC is out visiting more schools, then maybe the director will encounter these kinds of ignorant instructors. After all, this type of thought process is likely impacting our JROTC programs in a negative way by creating a negative culture.

Major Powers created a racist culture at the Lake Brantley JROTC program. So much so that some of the cadets were completely comfortable with calling me a Nigger, comfortable with saying that I needed to be tarred and feathered, and completely comfortable in using their real faces as avatars on their Instagram accounts as they spewed out their racist comments.

Every day around the country, tens of thousands of cadets recite the AFJROTC cadet creed. The AFJROTC cadet creed is very powerful and thought provoking, especially to a young person. The AFJROTC cadet creed is very different than all the other JROTC creeds. For starters, the Air Force JROTC creed uses the word "patriot" within its creed, whereas the other JROTC creeds don't use that word. All of the JROTC creeds use the words "patriotic" or "patriotism." I believe that it is important to stress the words "patriotic" and "patriotism" as they are part of the fabric of our country as well as the AFJROTC program. However, I am personally not a fan of the word "patriot" in describing an AFJROTC cadet. I believe that using the word "patriot" in the context of JROTC is questionable at best. After the January 6th, 2021 insurrection at our nation's capital, the word "patriot" caries a different meaning to many folks. Many of the individuals that stormed the U.S. Capital building called themselves "patriots" as they beat and pepper sprayed the heroic police officers that were simply trying to do their job and protect the capital. There must be a reason that the other services do not use the word "patriot' within their JROTC creed. In my opinion, it's because the word "patriot" has been corrupted and hijacked by extremists in our country.

AFJROTC CREED

I am an Air Force Junior ROTC Cadet. I am connected and faithful to every Corps of Cadets who served their community and nation with Patriotism. I earn respect when I uphold the Core Values of Integrity First, Service Before Self, and Excellence in All We Do. I will always conduct myself to bring credit to my family, school,

Corps of Cadets, community, and to myself. My character defines me. I will not lie, cheat, or steal. I am accountable for my actions and deeds. I will hold others accountable for their actions as well. I will honor those I serve with, those who have gone before me, and those who will come after me. I am a Patriot, a Leader, and a Wingman devoted to those I follow, serve, and lead. I am an Air Force Junior ROTC Cadet.

ARMY JROTC CREED

I am an Army Junior ROTC Cadet. I will always conduct myself to bring credit to my family, country, school and the Corps of Cadets. I am loyal and patriotic. I am the future of the United States of America. I shall not lie, cheat, or steal, and will always be accountable for both my actions and deeds. I shall always practice good citizenship and patriotism. I will work hard to improve my mind and strengthen my body. I will seek the mantle of leadership, be it civic or military, and stand prepared to uphold and defend the constitution and the American way of life. May God grant me the vigilance and prudence so that I may always live by this creed.

NAVY JROTC CREED

I am a Navy Junior ROTC Cadet. I strive to promote patriotism and to become an informed and responsible citizen. I respect those in positions of authority. I support those who have gone before me to defend freedom and democracy around the world. I proudly embrace the Navy's core values of Honor, Courage and Commit-

ment. I am committed to excellence and the fair treatment of all.

MARINE CORPS JROTC CREED

I am a Marine Corps Junior ROTC Cadet. I will always conduct myself to bring credit to my family, country, school, and the corps of cadets. I am loyal and patriotic. I am the future of the United States of America. I do not lie, cheat, or steal and will always be accountable for my actions and deeds. I will always practice good citizenship and patriotism. I will work hard to improve my mind and strengthen my body. I will seek the mantle of leadership and stand prepared to uphold the Constitution and the American way of life. May I possess the strength to always live by this creed.

COAST GUARD JROTC CREED

I am proud to be a United States Coast Guard JROTC Cadet. I revere that long line of splendid Coasties who by their devotion to duty and sacrifice, have made it possible for me to be associated with a service honored and respected throughout the world. I never, by word or deed, will bring disgrace upon the name of the U.S. Coast Guard. I will cheerfully fulfill my commitments and obligations and shall endeavor to do more, rather than less, than my share. I will always act with integrity and be respectful. I shall endeavor to be a model citizen in the community in which I live. I shall endeavor to be a noble work, living by the Coast Guard's Core Values, Honor Respect, and Devotion to Duty.

There is great opportunity available to make AFJROTC better. Yes, the word better is subjective. However, I feel that we should always strive for perfection. Like the cliché states, "It starts at the top." Coming out of the COVID-19 pandemic, our AFJROTC programs need a boost of adrenaline. We need strong guidance and leadership to get us back on track. It is my strong opinion that HQAFJROTC needs to form an advisory committee. To get some real input from the Air Force instructors who are out there in the field. We must find the negative trends in our programs and work to make them better while building on the positive trends.

Recently, the Director of the Air Force Junior ROTC was asked by an Associated Press reporter if he had anything to say about what happened with MSgt Hopkins at Lake Brantley, the Director would only say that he was aware of what had happened, but he deferred to the school for punishment and/or change in the program's status. In my opinion, that was the perfect time to get ahead of the controversy as did Lt. General Jay Silveria at the Air Force Academy when there was suspicious of racism at the Air Force Academy.

If I could speak directly to the new Director of the Air Force Junior ROTC, I would suggest that he add a "diversity" chapter or a chapter covering "tolerance, understanding and inclusion" to our Leadership Education textbook. I would remind him that AFJROTC is an awesome program. We all know the Air Force core values. The AFJROTC program is grounded in the Air Force core values of "integrity first, service before self, and excellence in all we do." Intolerance and racial division is not what the United States Air Force is about, and it should not be what AFJROTC is about. These core values don't end when we become AFJROTC instructors. If anything, this emphasis increases as we are charged with instilling values of citizenship, service to the United States, personal responsibility and sense of accomplishment in our cadets.

Sir, you are the Director of the Air Force Junior ROTC. You have the resources, the ability, and the power to fix this.

FIX IT!

AN INTERVIEW WITH DANIEL SMITH, TEACHER AND ADVOCATE

BY LIL BARCASKI CEO OF GWN PUBLISHING

Tell me a little a bit about who you are, Dan?

I'm Dan Smith, a Seminole County teacher since 2002 and presently I am out of the classroom to serve as President of the Seminole Education Association, the teacher's union for the teachers of Seminole County Public Schools.

How did you come to find out about what happened with Cardelle Hopkins at Lake Brantley HS?

I was contacted in January of 2020 by a guidance counselor at Lake Brantley High School, Vinette Young. Vinette was copied on the email that Sgt. Hopkins sent to Brian Blasewitz (Lake Brantley HS Principal). Vinette contacted me.

NO NIGGERS IN MY CORPS

> As president of the Seminole Education Association, I am a "release-time" employee, meaning that per our CBA, I continue to be a teacher-based employee with the district, but I am not a teacher assigned to a school, nor do I have students or a teaching schedule. The school I was assigned to before becoming president of the SEA was Lake Brantley HS. I have known Vinette for years, and she reached out to me.

> According to Vinette, (her words), "As a black woman, hearing what had occurred, I instantly felt sad for him. He represents the distaste that many Blacks have to endure." I personally think Vinette was holding back as "sad" does not even come close to what I felt when I heard – but I cannot put words in Vinette's mouth.

What was your reaction to the behavior of these students?

> On the one hand (my first reaction) was shock and outrage. After processing and reflection, my reaction was that I was not that surprised. Seminole County Public School District's priorities, in this order, are:
>
> 1. Not being sued
>
> 2. Not having any bad publicity
>
> 3. Serving the students of Seminole County
>
> My point being that SCPS has a habit of brushing these kind of issues "under the rug" as the district feels that any blemish that is publicized will reflect poorly on them as a district. As you well know, and as any person who has taken a 7th grade social studies class knows, ignoring the problems only feeds the problem and makes it larger.

An Interview with Daniel Smith, Teacher and Advocate

What do you think should have been done to rectify the situation in a more positive way?

The principal and the district, should really have listened to Sgt. Hopkins and taken his suggestions on how to rectify the problem. He was the victim, and his suggestion(s) were rooted in education, life lessons, and trying to bridge the divide between the perpetrators and the victim. He asked that a meeting with the students, their parents, and Lake Brantley's Administration take place to bring the issues out at a table to discuss and problem-solve. Sgt. Hopkins was not interested in having the students expelled from school – he wanted a learning experience, an opportunity to say – "this happened, and it was wrong. Let's discuss and resolve"

Cardelle Hopkins, as a gentleman, as a patriot, as a hero, DID NOT get angry at the district, did not threaten to bring a lawsuit against the district but instead, he did what any gentleman, patriot, hero would do in this situation. He tried to educate, inform, and maybe get students to see why it is wrong to do what they did. He is a better man than I am. I would not have acted so rationally. Not only were the actions by the students outrageous, but the district's position "not to draw attention" to the incident was even more outrageous because they are educated adults.

How do you see the future for students like this who feel they can treat a teacher and veteran this way?

Not good for any parties involved. When students choose to take the kind of action that they took against Sgt. Hopkins, these are students that need help. I do not know if they actually have hate in their hearts (Sgt. Hopkins does not think so, but I am not convinced) but after working with this age of students for 30 years, I know the students get these ideas and positions from home. I think the students who do these kind of things (as well as their parents) feel that they support our veterans – until – it becomes inconvenient for them. They support our veterans until it affects them in a bad way. Not a good look for our future.

The students who did this learned that they could do these hateful acts without consequence (I am not certain, but I think Cardelle told me the students got three days of OSS). That is the same punishment that a student can receive for getting caught smoking on campus. In a student's mind, transgressions without consequences are not transgressions at all – meaning they will continue to do as they please.

Additionally, beyond Cardelle Hopkins, SCPS ignores bad student behavior. When a student violates the district's Code of Conduct, the teacher uses various interventions to correct the behavior. Eventually, the teacher will write a discipline referral so the school's administration will deal with the student. In the past three years – the school's administration rarely deals with the student. They give the student a warning, a tootsie roll, and sends them back to class. The students have become empowered, and this inappropriate behavior is getting worse and worse each year. This lack of support from school administration has caused a massive exodus of our teachers leaving the district and teaching overall. As of today, we have had 219 teachers resign – during the school year. As our unit has approximately 4,600 teachers, this is approximately 5% of our unit.

Many times, when a student commits violations to the C of C, and a parent has some influence, they (the parent) will contact the school principal or a school board member and get the principal to get rid of the discipline referral. Lake

An Interview with Daniel Smith, Teacher and Advocate

Brantley HS has a lot of influential parents in their attendance zone – I taught there for 10 years before my current position. In 2017, I represented a Spanish teacher at Lake Brantley HS who had a different, but similar, incident. One of her students liked to "showboat" and would say in front of the class, "Are you a legal immigrant?" "Can I see your papers to prove that you are in this country legally?" The teacher tried to privately discuss the issue with the student but as that did not work, she had no choice but to write a discipline referral. When the parent found out, she was outraged and insisted the referral not be processed as it may stain the student's record when applying for colleges. The principal went to the teacher during one of her classes and asked that the referral not be processed.

I apologize for the political reference, but that attendance zone has a large amount of "Trumpers." I do not mean to claim that politics has anything to do with Cardelle's issue, but as a debate teacher at Lake Brantley, 2016 was one of my most difficult years. The students wore Trump on their sleeves and used the President's rhetoric during debates and class discussions.

NO NIGGERS IN MY CORPS

APPENDIX

Apology Letter 1

January 18th, 2020

Master Sergeant Hopkins,

When I reflect back on choices I've made in my lifetime, there are only a few that I regret. Going into my freshman year, I was nervous, hesitant, and scared for what it would bring me. I was young, dumb, and clueless. With family in the military or retired from, I was encouraged to take ROTC. I didn't really know what it was, and I was not expecting to enjoy it. My freshman year in ROTC began to teach me what it's like to work as a team; what it is like to be part of an organization that accepts you no matter what. ROTC welcomed me unlike any other team or organization I've been part of. Because I was so welcomed and eager to learn more, I signed up to take ROTC my Sophomore year. Unexpectedly, the Aerospace Science Instructor from my freshman year left, so he was replaced. Then came you. From the moment I met you my sophomore year, you had faith in me. You taught me lessons I never would've been taught had you not transferred her to Lake Brantley. You entertained my complaints and pointless arguments. You allowed me to prove myself and helped me grow out of my shell. ROTC my sophomore year was amazing and beneficial for the sole purpose of you. Sophomore year was a lot of work because I proved myself to you and the Senior Instructor that I was capable of being a leader; I was capable of being one to run the unit. Junior class registration came along and I without a doubt signed up for ROTC for my third year. I was told by many that I should shoot for deputy group commander, but I was scared. Deputy Group Commander seemed like a lot of work and time. Despite my fright, I continued to work hard and applied for Deputy Group Commander. To my surprise, I was selected to serve as Deputy Group Commander for my Junior Year. I was filled with a mixture of emotions: gratitude, fear, excitement, and most of all thankful. Without you as an instructor, I wouldn't have been brought out of my shell and taught the skills that I know now. The year ended strong and I was excited for what experiences my junior year would entail. Going into Junior year, I was nervous. This was the year of inspection, there was plenty of work to be done, and I was a junior thrown into the position. I had plenty to learn and despite my fear, you walked me through every step of the way. ROTC continued to be my safe haven and place of comfort. I was in ROTC as much as I could, and I was always working to make the unit the best it could be. Towards the beginning of the year, I started hanging out with some kids I shouldn't have. I started acting different and not focusing on things that I should have been focusing on. I continued to work hard, but deep down I was sad. I wasn't happy with myself or how I was behaving. My grades were slowly slipping because I paid more attention to texting what I thought were my best friends. I was procrastinating and avoiding work as much as possible. I was so angry with myself that I was letting it out on everyone around me, including the one person that taught me everything I know. The one person that made me who I am, who accepted me no matter what, who I consider to be a father figure. My vocabulary was expanded with words that shouldn't even be there. I started cursing more and I said words that I never would've thought to say if I would've stayed focused on school and the important things rather than friends and trying to be cool. I am not trying to make excuses for my actions and what I did because as you know, it was inexcusable and unacceptable. I was really angry when I saw how successful Seminole High School's ROTC was and the fact that they applied things successfully that you wouldn't let us try. My anger was expressed in ways that I was not raised to express them in. I *said things I shouldn't have said out of anger and frustration. I am disappointed in myself greatly and I deserve the punishment I got. This letter is not written to try to convince you to let me back in the program because I know I'm no longer welcomed. I gave away my welcome when I said words that I shouldn't have said, nor did I mean in any way. Because of my impulsive and stupid way of expressing my frustration, I am stripped of trust, respect, and thing that makes me the happiest, proudest, and best version of myself. I am not writing this to explain myself, because the statements I made give away their own explanation. I am not making excuses because I take full responsibility for what I said. I am deeply sorry, and I wish so badly that I could go back in time and take my words back and stop hanging around the wrong crowd. I have never regretted something so bad. I regret what I said, not that I got caught. Everything happens for a reason, I'm just not quite sure what this one is. Everything will work itself out, but I am really and truly sorry. What I said was wrong and I didn't mean a single word of it. I know I have lost all your respect and faith and I know I won't be getting it back. All I ask is that you read this and know that I am really sorry. I have never ever gotten in any trouble whatsoever. I have never acted like this before. This has taught me to not trust everyone; to focus on the important things instead of popularity and friends. If I had done so, I would not be in this horrible situation. As you may know, I was given three days of out-of-school suspension and I was removed from the ROTC program. I deserve any punishment I am given because that was not me; that was not something I would've ever done. I view you as a father figure; as someone who was always there for me and I was supposed to always be there for. ROTC was my safe haven and I loved being Deputy Group Commander with all my heart. It was one of the two things to bring me tremendous amounts of happiness. I let you down, MSgt. I'm disappointed and you have every right to be disappointed in me, too. I was taught my lesson the hard way and because of my poor teenager choices, I face the consequences. Please just know that you were the person to teach me the most valuable life lessons. If I had never met you, I wouldn't be the person I am today. Thank you for everything you've done for me and for this unit. I'm sorry for letting not only you down, but the unit down. I know things will never go back to the way they were, but I truly am sorry. I would like to talk to you in person, but I'm sure you don't want to talk. I really and truly do apologize MSgt.*

Sincerely,
█████████████

Appendix

Apology Letter 2

FROM: ███████████████████████

SENT: Wednesday, January 22, 2020

TO: Hopkins, Cardelle A. <hopkincz@scps.k12.fl.us>

SUBJECT: Important

Dear MSgt Hopkins,

During these past few days, regrettable events took place and I would like to explain my side of the story. I would like to apologize for what I said in this group chat; it was meant to be taken as a joke, not an offensive slur. I didn't make it out to hurt or offend you in anyway and I am truly sorry. I have nothing but the utmost respect for you and the things that you do for this unit; spanning from setting up events, running competitions, helping with our jobs, being a father figure, helping us grow, and always being there no matter what. It is truly a sacrifice when you give up your family time, drive over two hours everyday to get to our school and doing so with a positive attitude. I am honored to have been given a job on staff and a place in your heart. With that being said, I would like to offer my explanation of the why and what happened. In a group chat consisting of me and a group of my close friends from the corps, I said things that I shouldn't have regarding the use of the n-word. This was not meant to target you, as administration and the screenshots have demonstrated. It was meant to be taken as a joke, although racial terms are not a very good source of funny material, and I never meant to call you that. Part of my family is African American and this is how we joke around with each other. Usually, I don't think twice when making these jokes, and they aren't meant to be taken seriously or as a threat. Once again I am truly sorry for what I said and how I said it. This was a learning experience for me; I learned a valuable lesson, which is to think before you

NO NIGGERS IN MY CORPS

speak no matter what it is. I will make sure that this never happens again and I hope you can forgive for what happened, but I understand if you don't.

Sincerely,
██████████████

Appendix

EEOC form 5 Charge of Discrimination

EEOC Form 5 (11/09)	

CHARGE OF DISCRIMINATION

This form is affected by the Privacy Act of 1974. See enclosed Privacy Act Statement and other information before completing this form.

Charge Presented To:
- [ ] FEPA
- [X] EEOC

Agency(ies) Charge No(s): 02149

FLORIDA COMMISSION ON HUMAN RELATIONS and EEOC

State or local Agency, if any

Name (indicate Mr., Ms., Mrs.)
MR. CARDELLE A HOPKINS

Home Phone: [redacted]
Year of Birth: [redacted]

Street Address [redacted]
City, State and ZIP Code [redacted]

Named is the Employer, Labor Organization, Employment Agency, Apprenticeship Committee, or State or Local Government Agency That I Believe Discriminated Against Me or Others. (If more than two, list under PARTICULARS below.)

Name: SEMINOLE COUNTY PUBLIC SCHOOLS LAKE BRANTLEY HIGH SCHOOL
No. Employees, Members: 201 - 500
Phone No.: [redacted]

Street Address: 400 EAST LAKE MARY BOULEVARD, SANFORD, FL 32773

DISCRIMINATION BASED ON (Check appropriate box(es).)

- [ ] RACE
- [ ] COLOR
- [ ] SEX
- [ ] RETALIATION
- [ ] AGE
- [ ] DISABILITY
- [X] RELIGION
- [ ] NATIONAL ORIGIN
- [ ] GENETIC INFORMATION
- [ ] OTHER (Specify)
- [ ] CONTINUING ACTION

DATE(S) DISCRIMINATION TOOK PLACE
Earliest: 01-01-2020   Latest: 02-05-2020
[X]

THE PARTICULARS ARE (If additional paper is needed, attach extra sheet(s)):

I want this charge filed with both the EEOC and the State or local Agency, if any. I will advise the agencies if I change my address or phone number and I will cooperate fully with them in the processing of my charge in accordance with their procedures.

NOTARY – When necessary for State and Local Agency Requirements

I swear or affirm that I have read the above charge and that it is true to the best of my knowledge, information and belief.
SIGNATURE OF COMPLAINANT

Email to the Superintendent

FROM: ▮▮▮▮ <▮▮▮▮@scps.k12.fl.us>
SENT: Wednesday, January 15, 2020 5:20 PM
TO: Hopkins, Cardelle A. <hopkincz@scps.k12.fl.us>; ▮▮▮▮ <▮▮▮▮@scps.k12.fl.us>
CC: ▮▮▮▮ <▮▮▮▮@scps.k12.fl.us>
SUBJECT: Re: Identity Theft of JROTC Instructor

Mr. Blasewitz,

Please report this to your School Resource Officer. I will also alert my team.

▮▮▮▮ Ed.D.
Superintendent
Seminole County Public Schools

Sent from my iPad

On Jan 15, 2020, at 5:16 PM, Hopkins, Cardelle A. <hopkincz@scps.k12.fl.us> wrote:

> *Good Afternoon Mr. ▮▮▮▮,*
>
> *Today during lunch, two JROTC cadets showed me two fake Instagram accounts (see below). One of the fake accounts is posing as me. The other is supposed to be our JROTC unit. The account posing as me also has my school picture as its avatar. The second account has the official AFJROTC logo as its avatar. Both accounts are marked as "private." All of the members are JROTC cadets at LBHS except one. The problem is the accounts are both completely fake. I do not even own or have an Instagram account. Upon seeing the*

Appendix

accounts, I quickly contacted our School Resource Officer, Officer ▓▓▓▓. Although I was, and still am very angry, I did not attempt to engage the cadets associated with fake pages, as I wanted to completely be professional and allow the school to take the proper actions.

During my 23 years in the United States Air Force and also my time as a Juvenile Probation Officer in Hillsborough County, I have never experienced anything this flagrant as it pertains to an attack on my good name. Lake Brantley is a great school, and our ROTC program is outstanding. However, I am concerned that the creator(s) of the fake accounts may foolishly go too far and destroy my reputation and embarrass our school by publishing more fictious posts posing as me.

I am somewhat surprised that the cadets would be bold enough to use their actual Instagram accounts when they joined the two private groups. As you look at the members of the groups, you will quickly see that both groups have basically the same members, so there is a direct correlation between the two groups and the two Instagram pages. This leads me to believe that they all know who the creator(s) of the fake pages are.

I truly trust and respect Seminole County Public Schools (SCPS). Therefore, I am respectfully requesting that SCPS find and appropriately punish the individual(s) responsible for this action. However, I also have to try and protect and preserve my good name and reputation as well. So, should no action be taken on my behalf by SCPS, I plan on hiring a private investigator who specializes in internet fraud to figure out who created the fake page of me and posted the information posing as me. Thank you.

Respectfully,
Master Sergeant, Cardelle "Anthony" Hopkins, USAF (Ret.)
Air Force Junior ROTC Instructor
Aerospace Science Instructor/ASI
Lake Brantley High School
991 Sand Lake Rd, Altamonte Springs, FL 32714

Appendix

NO NIGGERS IN MY CORPS

Appendix

NO NIGGERS IN MY CORPS

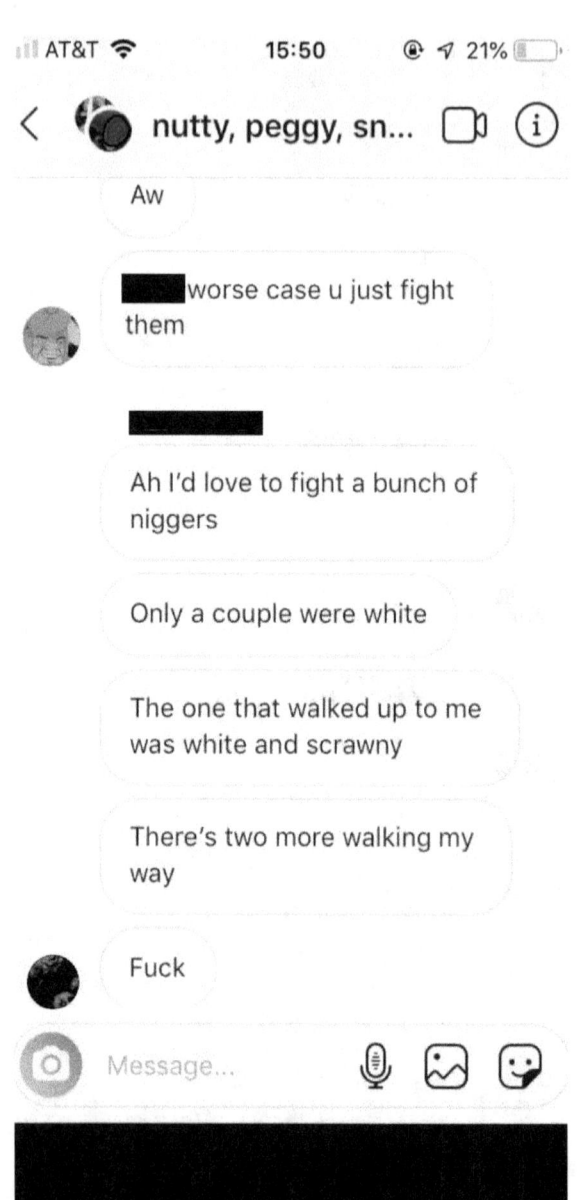

Appendix

> I'm telling you, I'm gonna quit and see him scramble for inspection

> I'm gonna tell him we want cadet ran

> If he completely steps back I told ▇▇▇ I've got dibs on MSgts desk and he can have colonels

> We can do a far better job working together without instructor assistance

> And if he continues and won't promise me changes for next year, I'll just be straightforward and say step down nigger

> Msgt can derank me or put me on probation or whatever but it won't bother me because rank means nothing

NO NIGGERS IN MY CORPS

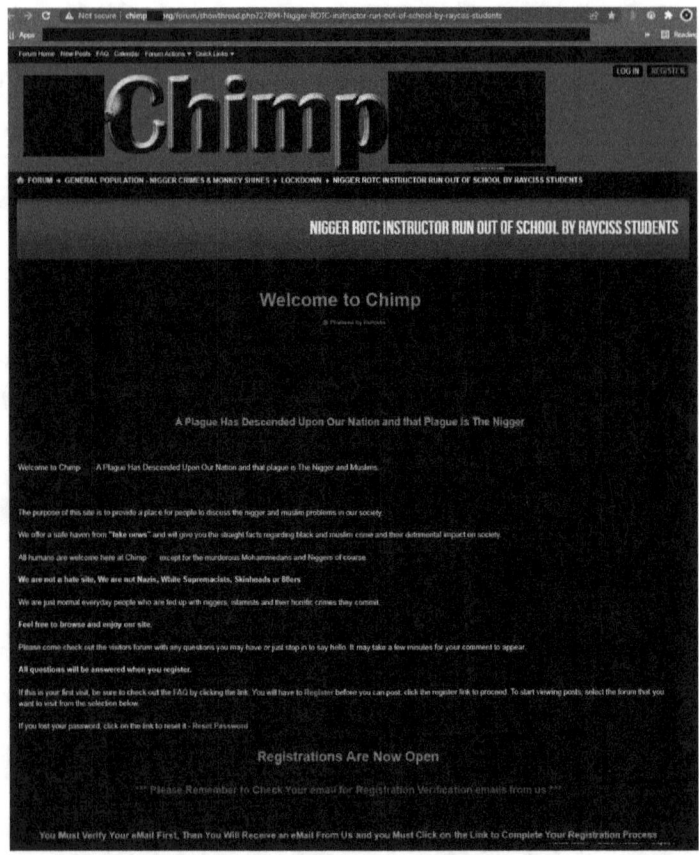

Appendix

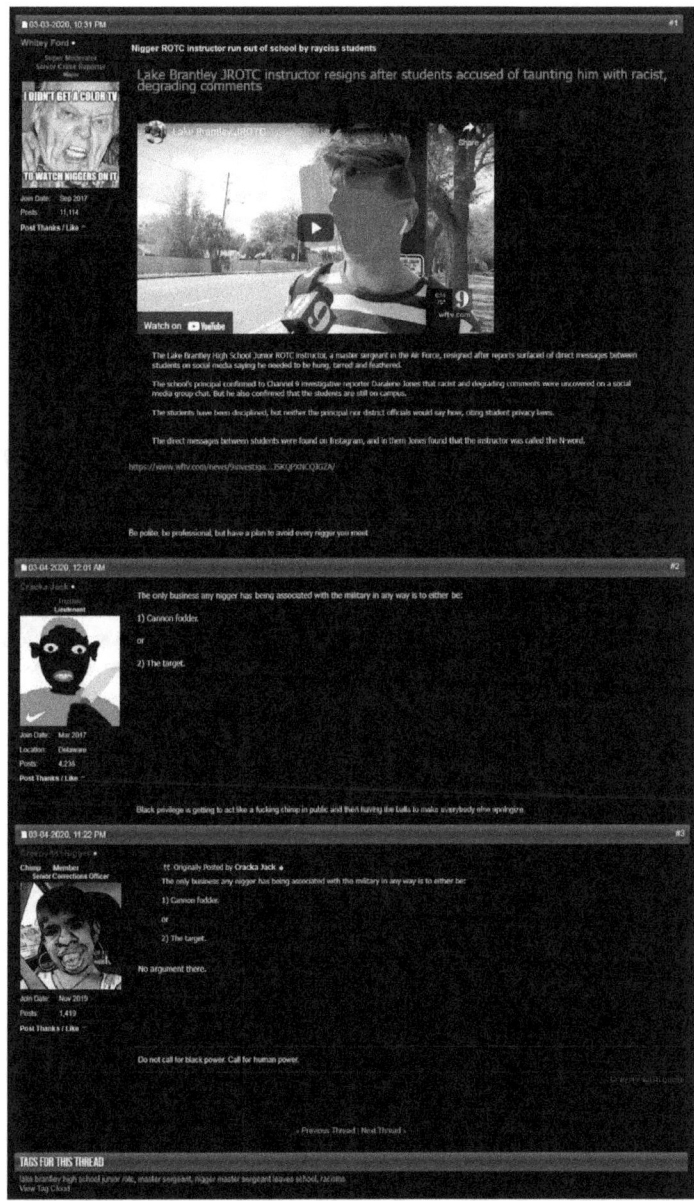

ACKNOWLEDGMENTS

I would like to thank Daralena Jones from Orlando news station WFTV, Channel 9. Daralena, the Emmy award-winning investigative reporter, broke the original story about the racist incidents that happened to me at Lake Brantley High School. Her thorough and detailed reporting brought tremendous attention to my situation.

I would like to thank Dan Smith, president of the Seminole Education Association. From the first conversation with Dan, he was very blunt in his take on racism. Dan's guidance and his knowledge of the history of race relations at Lake Brantley High School helped me better understand exactly what I was dealing with. He helped me better wade through the racial waters of being a black teacher at Lake Brantley High School.

I would also like to thank Noreen Nasir from the Associated Press. Noreen is a video journalist who covers stories in the United States and specializes in race and ethnicity. She is a consummate professional with vast experience. Noreen flew down to our home and spent several days with us interviewing me for a contribution to a three-part series on race in the

United States military. It was a pleasure working with her as she was very detailed and accurate in her reporting.

I want to thank Lil Barcaski of GWN Publishing and Virtual Creatives. I have never written a book before. Lil and her team guided me through the process. Lil was always available through email or text message anytime I had a question or an issue with the process. Although I had originally planned to work with another company to assist me in writing this book, I ultimately chose to work with Lil and her team. I am so grateful for Lil and her creative guidance!

Lastly, I want to thank the Hopkins and Garriga families, and all my friends for the support and encouragement y'all have given me throughout the years. Especially my two sons, Pep and AJ, you young men are my life! Thank you to M. Comas, A. Hattersley, P. Nicholson, and Dr. T. Daniel. Thank you to S.M. Lindsey for all the love and support. Many thanks to my brother and sister, Michael and Chrisanna for being there. Mom and Dad, I love you!

If I missed anyone, I deeply apologize.

ABOUT THE AUTHOR

Retired Master Sergeant Cardelle Anthony Hopkins spent 23 years in the United States Air Force. Cardelle enlisted in the Air Force at the Military Entrance Processing Stations (MEPS) in Columbia/Fort Jackson, South Carolina on April 4th, 1988. Cardelle married his wife, Michelle, in 1989 and they have two sons. During Cardelle's military career, he has been stationed at Lackland Air Force Base, Texas; Keesler Air Force Base, Mississippi; Sheppard Air Force Base, Texas; Incirlik Air Force Base, Republic of Turkey; Offutt Air Force Base, Nebraska; and Shaw Air Force Base, South Carolina. In 2000, Cardelle honorably separated from the USAF. He reentered the USAF in 2002 and was stationed at MacDill Air Force Base in Florida, where he later retired in 2013.

Cardelle earned a B.A. in Criminal Justice in 2016 with a minor in Homeland Security. Subsequently, he worked as a certified Juvenile Probation Officer (JPO) in the downtown Tampa, Florida field office. As a JPO, Cardelle was able to employ many of his mentoring skills that he learned from his years of experience in the military.

In 2017, Cardelle became a certified Air Force JROTC Instructor. He has had the opportunity to teach JROTC at three high schools. When not teaching, Cardelle can be found writing and producing music for his independent record label, Tampa Music Machine. Cardelle is also an avid Ford Mustang enthusiast. He and his two sons routinely frequent muscle car shows and meet-ups around the Tampa Bay area.

Cardelle is available for speaking engagements.

Contact Cardelle and learn more about him on his website, NONIMC.com

www.ingramcontent.com/pod-product-compliance
Lightning Source LLC
Chambersburg PA
CBHW051452290426
44109CB00016B/1728